# Emotional Connection
## *The EmC Strategy*

*How Leaders Can Unlock the Human Potential, Build Resilient Teams, and Nurture Thriving Cultures*

Lola Gershfeld and Ramin Sedehi

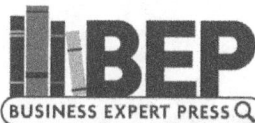

**BEP**

BUSINESS EXPERT PRESS
*Leader in applied, concise business books*

*Emotional Connection The EmC Strategy:*
*How Leaders Can Unlock the Human Potential, Build Resilient Teams, and*
*Nurture Thriving Cultures*

First published in 2021 by
Business Expert Press, LLC
222 East 46th Street, New York, NY 10017
www.businessexpertpress.com

ISBN-13: 978-1-63742-026-3 (paperback)
ISBN-13: 978-1-63742-027-0 (e-book)

Business Expert Press Human Resource Management and Organizational
Behavior Collection

Collection ISSN: 1946-5637 (print)
Collection ISSN: 1946-5645 (electronic)

First edition: 2021

10 9 8 7 6 5 4 3 2 1

# Description

Ann was agitated and troubled as she summoned the courage to recount what had happened. The intensity of her remarks was gripping the whole team; all eyes were on her. She took the extraordinary step of sharing her emotions with her team; she felt alone, helpless, unimportant, and rejected.

In reflecting on our individual professional experiences, we each remember occasions when we were Ann; desperate for connection. At times we reacted by retreating to our offices and at other times by becoming angry, shouting, or being overly defensive. Has this ever happened to you? Have you felt that emotions don't belong at work?

We assert that underlying all of our interactions are the emotions we are all operating with, both consciously and unconsciously. Emotions, and not the content, are the most powerful presence in the room during conflicts and stress. But knowing this is not enough.

This book lights the way to appreciating the importance of developing the emotional language to describe, acknowledge, and address emotions in the workplace using a proven and methodical approach absent in most other EI strategies. The EmC strategy will enable the leader inside you to connect more effectively, energize a harmonious workplace culture, and nurture creativity and innovation to achieve unprecedented results.

- Invigorate creativity, innovation, and collaboration
- Boost engagement and wellness
- Build psychological safety to enhance trust and authenticity
- Nurture leadership throughout the organization
- Foster strong relationships to create a thriving culture

Enduring relationships give us the strength to face volatility, uncertainty, complexity, and adversity. When we are connected, we can thrive, we can achieve unimaginable success.

# Keywords

emotional intelligence; emotional connection; conflict management; conflict resolution; workplace conflict; leadership development; leadership training; change management; team building; team engagement; building trust; psychological safety; workplace culture; company culture; team dynamics; emotional health; leadership; relationships; workplace relationships; team engagement; board engagement; emotional education; quality of life; fun at work; transparency; productivity; diversity; inclusion; enthusiasm; work environment; motivation; creativity; innovation; collaboration; thriving culture; business success; volatility; stress; work stress

# Emotional Connection
*The EmC Strategy*

# Contents

# Why Read This Book?

Have you ever known a team whose members just seem to get stuck—and cannot produce results the way you know they should?

Do some team members spend too much time arguing, or do some members simply withdraw?

Does the team lack enthusiasm and cohesiveness, with everyone pulling in a different direction?

Or, is your team okay, but not outstanding? Do you want to take their performance to the next level and beyond?

This book will show you how your teams can overcome these kinds of problems. You will understand how to help team members work more harmoniously, more effectively, and achieve more powerful results.

You will learn:

- A unique approach to solving age-old problems of conflicts at work—which are far too often only tolerated or ameliorated
- The psychological dynamics of human attachment and emotional connection and how they play out in the workplace and with teams
- How to analyze emotional interactions within a group and between group members
- Why some teams get stuck—and what to do about it
- How a team leader and team members can productively respond to emotions
- How to understand the language of emotions, triggers, and automatic responses
- Why nurturing emotional connections is also vital for leaders
- How to address common challenges that teams encounter—and turn them to your advantage

- What EmC means for the future of team performance
- Insights from team leaders who have successfully used the EmC process to solve problems and supercharge their team
- How to lead effectively using the EmC strategy to build strong communities and thriving cultures

# Foreword

We are living in one of the most unsettling periods in recent history. Nationally and internationally, as people, as businesses, and as institutions, we face a great deal of uncertainty and volatility. People everywhere report personal and professional anxiety, internal turmoil as to their present situation, and fear for a future that may be quite different from the one they had once imagined or prepared for. This book is for everyone who wishes to understand and exercise the power of emotional connections to pivot teams and organizations toward thriving.

My colleague, Dr. Gershfeld, shares with the reader the culmination of her work in the field of human connection, propitious in its timing and critical to our well-being. The Emotional Connection (EmC) strategy is academically sound, research-informed, and experiential in its methodology to restore the human connections necessary for people to engage, create, explore, and grow at work.

In this book, we intend to fundamentally shake the pillars upon which we interrelate with people at work. For the most part, we have been taught that the company is a place where relationships are transactional, dispassionate, and result-oriented. Moreover, emotions, we are told, have little to no place in the office. We assert that underlying all of our interactions are the emotions with which we are all operating, both consciously and unconsciously. Emotions are inherently present in the office, they impact everything we do, and the business results we are so keenly seeking can only come about when people are connected at an emotional level.

This book lights the way to appreciating the importance of developing the emotional language to describe, acknowledge, and address emotions within our workplaces. It is, and I can attest, a reprogramming of sorts, we are all capable of undergoing, but until now, we have not had the method to do so, competently and effectively. I remember her first words to me when I described a professional conflict that was quite troubling for me. As I tried to dig deeper into the content of the matter, as we all want to do, she stopped me. I had jumped headfirst into analyzing the content and the behaviors of everyone involved. She asked me instead to explore my emotions and what I was feeling at the time.

I must admit that it was the first time I had been asked to reflect on the emotions in such an extensive and systematic manner. I even remember being a bit irritated at the focus on emotions; it seemed unnatural for discussing a workplace conflict. The process slowly guided me to understand how I had become emotionally unbalanced during the conflict, how my reactions were understandable given the underlying emotions, and how it is that I can begin to find my way back to a place of balance.

I have come to learn that it is *not* the content that drives most conflicts, but rather the emotions that have been triggered and the cycle of negative events that follow, automatically and with consistency, they widen the rift, making it difficult to reconcile.

This reprogramming of our managerial brain to move away from the content and move toward a better understanding and acknowledging of emotions is a critical first step. We not only have a better chance of resolving conflicts; most importantly, we can build enduring bonds that become essential to achieving ambitious business goals.

Extraordinary results can only come from people who are thriving, and the key to that is emotional connection, where trust is high, values are aligned, and people feel valued by each other. The concepts of emotional connection, vulnerability, and attachment are well documented and discussed in various forums, books, articles, and programs. The EmC strategy has effectively consolidated the body of knowledge in this field into a purposeful and deliberate pathway to achieving the connection we all crave to thrive at work.

The EmC strategy teaches individuals that disconnections are inevitable, but the time we spend in cycles of negative thought and action is entirely controllable by us. If there is one thing that stands out in this work is that it is not a guarantee or a full-proof methodology, but rather a deeply personal process, a conversation, and an experience, which puts the principles of the conflict into direct engagement with each other. The learning that takes place is permanent and positive, both at work and at home. I am delighted that we are also able to share with you the importance of nurturing emotional connections for those who exercise or wish to exercise leadership.

Leadership is an entirely different proposition than management, as it is a state of being and not merely a role or a position. Leaders put themselves in the crosshairs of problems, out of moral, social, or personal obligations, creating an authentic experience for all those around them. Leaders naturally understand the power of connection in invoking the sense of purpose in themselves and others. They are driven by needs that are not so easily achievable or solvable. This book is essential reading to help leaders foster the courage necessary to move the needle, connect through compassion that accepts people as they are, and create environments where people feel emotionally safe, thereby boosting creativity.

In this year of ever-changing threats and societal angst, we are at another *stormy present*, as President Lincoln referred to a time of significant change in the United States after the civil war. The storm that is gathering around us is fierce and unrelenting; it is shattering our norms and our stability. But, as with all storms, they pass at some point, showing us a new path. Whatever form that new normal takes, we know it will be enlightened through human connections, authenticity, and vulnerability. It paves the way for us to expect the most from each other and ourselves, thus building strong and enduring relationships.

The richness of exploring our emotions and our connections may seem at first glance as local in its significance, but it seems to me that our collective humanity is at stake. Our bonds with each other are the vital building blocks of a new future at work, home, and as a global community.

Ramin Sedehi

# How to Use This Book

This book contains the science behind emotional connection, methodology for everyday interactions and strategic ramifications for management and leadership.

Some readers who choose to understand the background science and implications of the EmC strategy as it pertains to leadership and team performance would do well to focus on the following chapters:

- Chapter 1: Introduction into the World of Team Dynamics
- Chapter 2: Attachment in the Workplace
- Chapter 3: How Responses Are Shaped: The Power of Connections
- Chapter 8: Forming a Holistic Strategy Through EmC
- Chapter 9: How to Address Common Challenges
- Chapter 10: Team Resilience and Thriving Cultures

In addition to the preceding, for readers who wish to engage the methodology of the EmC process in detail, the following chapters delve deeply into the specifics of the Process and the reconnection post-conflict:

- Chapter 4: Exploring Emotions
- Chapter 5: From Being Stuck to Moving On
- Chapter 6: Are You There for Me?: The Magic of A.R.E.
- Chapter 7: How to Respond To Emotions

# Acknowledgments

To begin with, Lola thanks her clients with whom she had the honor to work over the past 10 years. They have trusted, captivated, and taught her. In the moments of vulnerability and tension in each session, she learned the reality of what it meant to be courageous and strong in order to repair, rebuild, and reconnect with their teams at a deeper level. Their courage has been an inspiration to Lola's commitment and dedication to her work.

In turn, Ramin is grateful to a great many colleagues throughout the various institutions with whom he shared the difficult as well as triumphant moments of accomplishing great deeds. It was the emotional connection and strong bonds that allowed these teams to achieve unprecedented results and, moreover, withstand the many storms they endured. Leadership thoughts and organizational concepts brought into this book would not have been possible without the many lessons from his mentors.

It is essential to recognize and appreciate the pioneers of this field, the great social psychologists, particularly Dr. Mario Mikulincer, Dr. Phil Shaver, and Dr. Sue Johnson. They performed the seminal work of applying the attachment theory to adult relationships and paving the way for us to share the Emotional Connection (EmC) process. Over the past 30 years, they have expanded the research and provided insights and knowledge, which we have used in working with teams. The EmC process would not exist without the work of these exceptional and dedicated professionals. A special thanks to Nienke van Bezooijen and Kimberly Goh for their intensive work on developing the online EmC training program and bringing it to life.

A special thanks to Edward Stone and Dan Hyun for valuable feedback and support to keep us focused and moving forward. We are grateful for their expertise and advice.

We are grateful for having literally bumped into each other while running and stopping to start a conversation that has led to a year-long partnership and a fantastic journey. This book is a culmination of our thoughts, practices, and expertise to help people build strong bonds at work and for leaders to truly unleash the power of their teams.

As with all efforts, this book could not be brought to completion without the support and commitment of Lola's husband, Jack, who is truly her rock and her inspiration. As for Ramin, it is his dear friends, Pat and Soha, who have taught him the power of positive relationships. We are truly in their debt.

# Lola's Thoughts

"There has to be a better way!" I remember saying these words to myself after yet another board meeting, which I felt was unproductive. We were clearly not hearing each other, the emotions in the room were overwhelming, and we were not getting anywhere in our approach.

I am writing this book because 10 years ago, I took steps to understand what was going on with me and all the other people on the board, as well as the problems I was encountering in various companies and teams. The process, outlined in this book, is my approach to solving age-old problems of conflicts and disconnections at work, which are far too often tolerated or ameliorated but are not solved!

While the actual process of resolving deep conflicts requires practice and expertise, every person working in any organization can learn the emotional vocabulary that exists for them and others and change the dynamics of negative conversations. This emotional language is missing in a lot of training programs and discussions at work.

My goal with this book is to help the reader understand that emotions are always present, whether at work or home. Understanding emotions and your response to them, clarifying your needs, and acknowledging the difficulty of the same task for others will help you navigate your next conflict.

The term conflict is used throughout the book. Conflicts are more than face-to-face disagreements, they are also results of stressful situations, disengagement from the workplace, low productivity, and lack of trust. I hope you will come to appreciate that it is possible to reverse these negative situations and create a more cohesive work environment. The roadmap in this book will serve as your guideline to understanding yourself and others, building the opportunity to form stronger, more resilient relationships and teams.

This book provides you with both the science of attachment as well as the knowledge of the EmC process. The real-life examples, which are drawn from a decade of practice, will provide you with a practical understanding of the EmC process.

It is my expectation that this book will inspire the leader in you to appreciate the importance of being emotionally connected with all whom you work with and to engage everyone in building and fostering communities of trust, capable of achieving great outcomes.

In these settings, people grow, thrive, and blossom.

Lola Gershfeld

# Overview of the Emotional Connection (EmC) Strategy

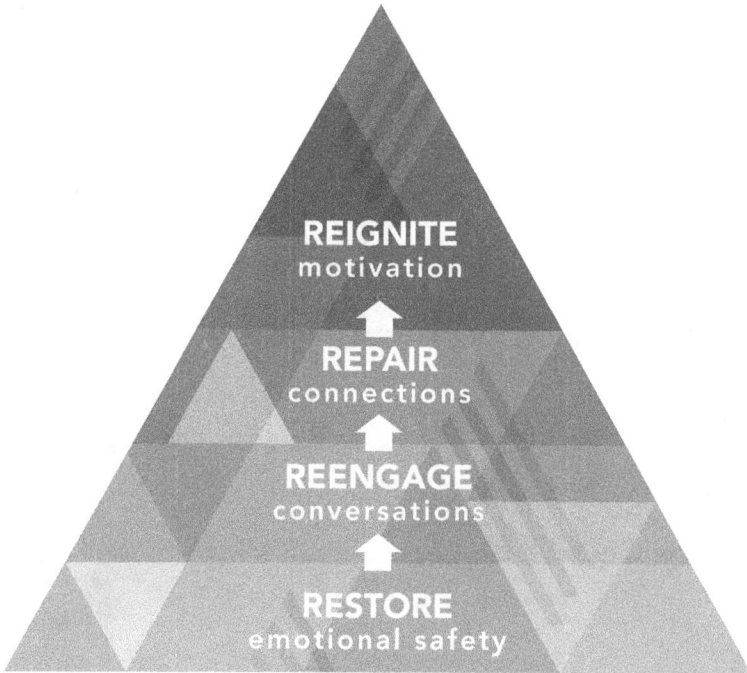

Figure 1.1 *Overview of the EmC Strategy*

# Overview of the Three Stages of the EmC Process

The Emotional Connection (EmC) process consists of three stages: de-escalate conflict, restructure the current interactions, and integrate new learnings and feelings (safety, Emotional Connection), and bonding conversations into daily interactions. See Figure 1.2.

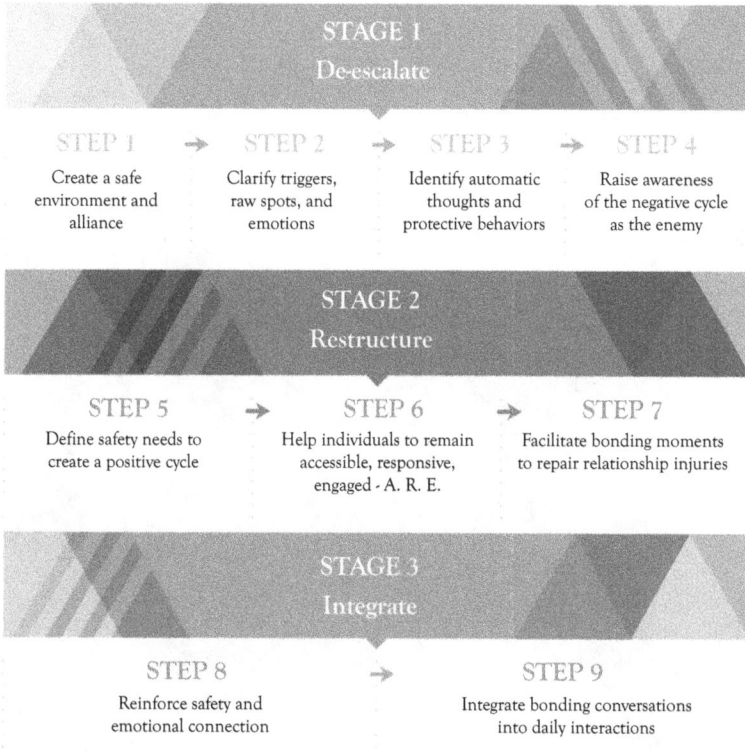

| STAGE 1 De-escalate | | | |
| --- | --- | --- | --- |
| STEP 1 → | STEP 2 → | STEP 3 → | STEP 4 |
| Create a safe environment and alliance | Clarify triggers, raw spots, and emotions | Identify automatic thoughts and protective behaviors | Raise awareness of the negative cycle as the enemy |

| STAGE 2 Restructure | | |
| --- | --- | --- |
| STEP 5 → | STEP 6 → | STEP 7 |
| Define safety needs to create a positive cycle | Help individuals to remain accessible, responsive, engaged - A. R. E. | Facilitate bonding moments to repair relationship injuries |

| STAGE 3 Integrate | |
| --- | --- |
| STEP 8 → | STEP 9 |
| Reinforce safety and emotional connection | Integrate bonding conversations into daily interactions |

Figure 1.2  Overview of the three stage in the EmC process

# CHAPTER 1

# Introduction into the Dynamics of Human Connection

Thriving teams are easy to spot. They are made of individuals with high levels of trust who have emotional safety within their organizations to be vulnerable and, thus, authentic.[1] This allows them to fully appreciate and support each other through the strong bonds they have built, using their unique abilities to deliver innovative and creative solutions to unprecedented problems. These teams function at high levels of performance, seemingly unlimited in their capacity to meet uncertainty and volatility in the business world.

This book is focused ultimately on helping you build and nurture a thriving culture that extends to all the individuals in your organization. Their ability to have positive relationships with each other and the organization's hierarchy are the bedrock of a flourishing business. There are many books, training programs, and courses to help teams achieve higher levels of performance; however, in our experience working with hundreds of people, the results are often temporary, leading to frustration and setbacks. The primary reason behind the frustration felt by leaders and teams using the current approaches is that most programs are either cognitively based, which focus on the content, or are behaviorally based, which focus on individual behaviors. In this book, we will show you a different and more effective way to deal with workplace conflict, team dynamics, and build relationships that provide resilience—ensuring creativity and strong performance.

Human beings naturally form strong emotional connections or *bonds* with each other, and this is very important in teams. In a healthy team, the members support each other and can accomplish magnificent results. But, team leaders and members must understand how to nurture their relationships and bonds so that when problems arise, they are able to deal with them in a productive and transparent manner. Insights from psychology about the impact we have on each other when we work together and the importance of adult bonding can provide the skills to supercharge team performance.

## Why Do Teams Struggle?

We have observed that struggling teams are often fraught with numerous conflicts, many of which have gone unresolved. Conflicts are deeper than arguing or disagreeing; they are symptoms of emotional disconnection and injured relationships. When unresolved at their roots, conflicts result in unproductivity, lack of accountability, project delays, and physical health problems, demonstrated by higher sick calls.

According to one study, 85 percent of the employees deal with conflict at some level during the workday, and it is estimated that 360 billion U.S. dollars in paid hours are lost each year to workplace conflicts.[2] Conflict at work is real, and it is worth solving permanently not just for the health of the individuals, but also for the health of the bottom line. To understand why we respond emotionally to each other, causing and inflating conflicts, we have to understand our innate need for attachment. Attachment is defined by psychologists as our need for continuous connection with whom we depend on. We are wired to be connected and struggle when we are not.[3] Solitary confinement is considered unusually harsh, as it deprives individuals from connections with others for long periods of time.

In evolutionary terms, emotion has acted as our alarm system. Emotion comes from the Latin word *emovere,* which means to move. If we think about it, emotion tells us what matters. It steers us toward what is worthwhile and away from danger. Emotions are contagious. Psychologists have found that we actually simulate the emotions we see other people experiencing. In fact, scientists have also discovered intriguing evidence that we have mirror neurons that fire when we see and experience emotion, helping us to mirror and feel the emotions we observe others exhibit.[4] Emotions that turn on our panic button are triggered by incongruences in our environment and give us the message that something is disconnected in our interaction with people we depend on. The key is, the people we depend on are our lifeline to our success, and we are the same for their success.

During the time we lived in caves, our tribe was there for hunting and safety; our quick responses were crucial to surviving: eat or be eaten. The way our brains are wired has not changed. Even though there are no longer saber-toothed tigers, our brains respond the same to panic or stress. While our work environment is no longer in caves, we consider those whom we work with as members of our tribe, thus depending on each other in times of stress. If we do not work well together, we are stuck, and we cannot move forward with our projects. Because of our dependency on each other, our brains become hypersensitive in our interactions with any type of signal, whether facial, verbal, or physical, that sends the message of disapproval, rejection, or disconnection.

When we have a strong connection, or what we call a secure attachment, our brain is less sensitive and less reactive to the changes in our interactions. For example, if a teammate or a boss does not respond to us when we expect it, our brain does not go into a panic. It says, "It's okay, I had many experiences with this person when he or she was there for me. The person is probably busy." However, if we have a weak connection or insecure attachment, our brain is vigilant and a lot more sensitive to these changes in our interaction. We say, "You see? I am not important to this person, and they don't care about me." or we say, "Oh my goodness, I have done something wrong; my boss is probably upset with me." This response happens automatically because the connection is not secure, and how does the brain respond when there is a change? It presses the panic button and goes into a survival mode—fight, flight, or freeze. The whole point of learning about emotions is to understand that they send us cues about the state of our connections. As humans, our ecological niche is to be a member of one or more groups of people. That is how we have been able to survive so well as a species. We both help and depend on each other.[5]

## Emotional Bonding Vital to Human Survival

Being bonding animals (meaning we form strong, lasting emotional attachments or connections with each other) was vital to our survival because we have the most vulnerable offspring of any species on Earth. A human child is completely helpless for the first six months and unable to fend off any predators. That fact and our need for care—to get a response from those we depend on—has structured our nervous system. Furthermore, it has a massive impact on how our biology works. For example, if we think of someone we have an emotional bond with, our body produces the bonding hormone, oxytocin, which calms us down, gives us emotional balance, and opens us up for social interaction. It makes us less afraid and more open to exploring. Because we evolved to be bonding animals, we depend on our team members and look for specific responses from them. That, in turn, impacts the way we engage, perform, and collaborate.

By learning how to recognize these cues and knowing how to address emotions, we can slow down the process before the brain presses the panic button. How great would it be if we could all recognize the patterns in our emotional responses before we press the panic button? It would save us so much time and the pain of disconnection. If we look at children, we observe how open they are to express their emotions explicitly and clearly. As adults, we have learned to protect ourselves by hiding our emotions. The better we are at this, ironically, the more we stand to create and feed conflicts, ultimately leading to disconnections. How does this relate to teams?

## Understanding Emotions: A Roadmap to Team Success

Understanding our emotional responses, patterns, and behaviors provides us with a roadmap for team success. It helps us know what team members need to feel safe and connected, how to coach them, how to understand what is happening when they feel vulnerable and threatened, and how to lead the team members into having a more cohesive and secure connection with each other. Also, it gives us insight into where teams get stuck. It helps us learn what team members do to create patterns of interaction that are positive or negative. A positive pattern of interaction can lead a team into a more secure bond with each other, while a negative pattern can lead the team into a state of perpetual emotional disconnection.

## What Is Attachment, and Why Must We Understand It First?

"What should we call this?" John Bowlby, a famous psychiatrist, having studied emotionally disturbed children at a London clinic, was sharing with his wife the theory he had formulated about what was missing in the children's lives that caused their psychological problems.

She responded, "You should call it a theory of love."

Deciding that it was too controversial, he called it, the Attachment Theory.[6] Bowlby defined attachment as a "lasting psychological connectedness between human beings."[7]

To develop a good team, we must understand the concepts of the attachment theory and the science of emotional connection. Bowlby discovered that people need secure emotional attachments to be healthy. These bonds start with the child's connection with the mother and other care providers, but they continue to be important after the child becomes an adult. Our need to bond continues into our adulthood and our workplace. The bond among team members is nurtured through positive emotional feedback loops, giving us information as to how we feel about each other, especially during times of stress. The attachment theory explains how our internal emotions affect our interactions with others and how the patterns of those interactions affect an essential part of our self. It also explains how we regulate our emotions and the emotional signals we send to other people.[8]

Other researchers built on Bowlby's work and have expanded our understanding of the science of emotional connection. The attachment theory was quickly complemented by the addition of humanistic theory, systems theory, and experiential theory to help us understand and describe emotions, work with emotions, and create the roadmap for the process of reconnection. Humanistic psychologist Carl Rogers, who revolutionized psychotherapy with his concept of *client-centered therapy*, stressed the importance of having unconditional positive regard and unrelenting empathy—and the fact that we have an innate ability to grow and develop. To establish a healthy emotional connection with each other, team members need to experience empathy and demonstrate an empathic response toward others.[9] Salvador Minuchin, a psychiatrist who radically changed the approach to family therapy, studied family systems. Minuchin revealed that families are systems whereby each member has an impact on the whole. An intervention must involve the whole system in order to be effective. In a family or a group or a team, when one member is stuck, the entire team is affected and is constricted and rigid. It cannot move forward and adapt to a new environment.[10]

Positive emotional connections create and restore the team's flexibility, enhancing its ability to adapt and deal with external and unforeseen changes. Fritz Perls and his wife Laura Perls were originators of the experiential theory in psychology. The key concept that was taken from their theory is *experience*; in the process of emotional connection, the goal is to be in the moment, to be fully in the present.[11] That is why, the key question is always: *What is happening with you at this moment?* Because when we can address the present emotion—what we are actually experiencing right now, we can experience the core attachment needs and what is needed to restore a healthy emotional connection. This process helps us be clear on our message to each other and what we need from each other to feel safe and comfortable.

## What Must Team Members Learn?

As with couples, team members work well together when they learn to become accessible and responsive to each other. They must learn how to recognize emotions, recognize when they get emotionally disconnected from each other, and understand that being disconnected is dysfunctional. In teams, recognizing the underlying emotions and resulting disconnections is an important step to changing the whole dynamic and repairing bonds that are needed for teams to be functional. But, repairing those bonds requires a special process, which we introduce to you in this book. It is a process intended at repairing and building strong emotional connections. The Emotional Connection (EmC) process is built on the foundation of the scientific work on attachment and years of on-the-ground experiential learning through working with clients in multiple industries. The EmC process helps create the language of saying what we really feel, more authentically expressing our emotions, helping us to connect with others, and nurture the relationships that we need to make flourish. People with high levels of emotional responsiveness are better able in general to function well in society and develop successful personal relationships of all kinds, including in teams.[12]

## Making Space for Expressing Emotions

Let us return from the theoretical background to daily reality with teams. If you think about your team and how you communicate, is there any space for the expression of emotions? In most businesses and organizations, the predominant subject of communications is content-based as it should be. Fortunately, thanks to Daniel Goleman[13] and others, the concept of emotional intelligence at the workplace has taken center stage as candidates are evaluated and individual performance is measured. However, while arguably we have a greater number of emotionally competent people at companies, the concept of emotion-based connections within teams and within individuals during times of stress and conflict is poorly understood and not well recognized. The lack of such recognition creates an environment promoting significant disconnections and a ripple effect leading to poor team performance. Here is an example of the disconnection and its ripple effect.

Linda, a director of the Western Region for Alfa Insurance Company, called Lola to help Linda with her team. She has been leading this team for 11 years as their director. They have worked closely together and have gone through a lot, but recently, Linda was furious about her team's behavior. She was going on a trip, and it was really important for the whole team to be at the meeting before her departure. She explained to Lola that two of her vice presidents did not show up at the conference call that was very important to her. Here is how the rest of the conversation went as Linda explained what happened:

> I mean, how can they do that? Who do they think they are? I was really furious, so I changed the rules and told them that from now on, we have to meet weekly. I mean, what was I supposed to do? If they don't respect my requests, I'll make more rules. I can't believe they didn't show up, and they knew how important this was for me. I mean, I've been going through a rough time, personally, and they all know that if they are so blind not to see how important this is for me, oh well! I mean, if we're not there for each other, how is this reflecting on the rest of the organization!

We will be examining Linda's team and the reconnection process throughout the rest of this book. The initial takeaway for this chapter is that her disproportionate response and the decision to hold more frequent meetings created an immediate panic among her team members. As a result, disconnections occurred between her and each team member as well as between the team members themselves. The ripple effect of this one simple disconnection permeated the entire organization, and for the five weeks before the formal intervention, it stifled their communications and interactions. In the next chapter, we will dive further into the first steps of how the EmC process works.

## Emotional Connection Starts With You!

In every chapter of this book, we invite you to experience the process of EmC through examples in your work relationships. EmC starts with yourself first. A critical aspect of experiencing this process involves reflecting on your thoughts, feelings, and reactions as you go through this book.

## Some Questions for Reflection

Here are some important questions for further reflection:

1. When interactions go wrong between you and your team or within members of your team, are there any specific patterns that you recognize or are able to outline?
2. What happens to you when the interaction goes wrong? Do you shut down or pursue the resolution? How do members of your team react in similar negative interactions with their colleagues?
3. Do you feel safe to share your answers to these questions with others?

## Summary of Chapter 1

In this chapter, the process of connection was discussed through an evolutionary perspective, attachment theory, family systems theory, as well as the contextual perspective of our modern work world. Evolutionarily, we are wired to respond quickly to stress and danger. In our caveman time, we knew exactly how we could count on one another. In those days, our mammalian brain made us feel safe and protected us from danger, which helped us to survive. As a tribe, we stayed connected and relied on each other naturally. As humans, our ecological niche has been to be a member of one or more groups. That is how we have been able to survive so well as a species. We both help and depend on each other.

Nowadays, our environment has changed, but the way our brain responds to stress and danger have not. Our tribe is now our team, our family, our peers, and others in our professional and personal communities. From our emotions and longing for a connection, we respond to each other throughout the day. The connection is an essential element in our ability to form positive and productive relationships at work, enabling outstanding team performance.

# CHAPTER 2

# Attachment in the Workplace

Most people shy away from wanting to understand their emotions, especially if they have experienced a great deal of emotional pain or conflict in their past. As a result, workplace conflicts center unproductively on the content of the conflict as opposed to the emotional underpinnings of the interactions. We must begin to understand our emotions and the strategies we have adopted for managing them in order to have safe and effective interactions during times of difficulty. Emotions tell us what matters, and ignoring them prevents us from moving forward. The strategies we learned as children to handle our emotions often carry forward to adulthood. Unfortunately, those strategies do not work as adults.

To understand our current response, let us take a closer look at what we learned as children. When we got hurt as children, emotionally or physically, we learned to run, freeze, or fight to protect our emotions and our view of ourselves. We picked a run, freeze, or fight strategy to soothe ourselves and to recover. Or, we cried when we were really hurt and overwhelmed. If we had a caregiver who created a safe space for us, we turned to the caregiver for comfort and support. That sense of safety helped us form a secure attachment and a felt sense of comfort that allowed us to take risks and engage in new experiences. The reassurance we received from our caregiver carries to our adulthood. It translated into our work environment by seeking secure emotional attachment with our teams, co-workers, and bosses.

When we work together, we depend on each other. This dependency creates a need for attachment and triggers our human desire to bond with people on our team. Emotional connection is the glue that holds the bond.

## Attachment Styles

In working to create or repair emotional bonds between team members or employees, it is important to note the different ways people deal with attachment problems. Often, these styles are carryovers from the strategies they used to deal with similar problems when they were children. But, as it has been noted, those strategies do not work so well for us as adults and can cause problems in teams and in working with others. People with a *secure attachment style* feel self-confident, and they openly communicate how they feel about things. They seek out and listen to others' feelings about problems and emotional connection issues. They exhibit what is called *constructive* or *effective dependency*, which is vital for teams, employees, and companies to function properly. We will learn more about that later in this chapter.

*The avoidant dependency style* uses a withdrawer's approach. To preserve whatever connection is left, withdrawers avoid confrontations, hesitate to share emotions, may spend a lot of time in their office behind a closed door, or, at times, act in an aggressive manner. They do not feel comfortable asking for help or turning to others in times of need. They often describe their strategy this way: "I don't need anything from anyone. Time will fix things. I just need to put my head down and do my work." These strategies leave withdrawers feeling alone and isolated and often result in alienation and significant frustration in others.

The *anxious* or *pursuer dependency style* feels insecure about their emotional connection with people they depend on, and their anxiety about this insecurity makes them pursue the connection. They often come across as demanding or aggressive in their pursuit, which threatens the withdrawers and results in people feeling intimidated and overwhelmed.[1] As an example, we are both pursuers. When we first started to learn about our attachment styles, we began to notice that the behaviors we used to protest the disconnect were often through blaming, judging, criticizing, and demanding. These are common behaviors that protect us during disconnects. We became aware that we were scaring people and not gaining the team results we had in mind. That feeling led to even more pursuing from our side in our respective situations, similar to the example of Linda's behavior we discussed in Chapter 1. As we became more aware of our emotions, we were able to soften our approach and use behaviors that helped others feel safe and for us to be more successful in seeking the connection. The same awareness on the part of the withdrawers on our individual teams allowed them to become more engaging. The safer we felt in articulating our emotions, the more engaged we became with our team members, thus improving our connection.

The key point is that both withdrawers and pursuers take these actions in order to protect the relationship and not to destroy it. The dysfunction is seemingly content-related, and while the importance of content should not be understated, it is the need to connect that is feeding the conflict and manifesting the negative behavior of protection. The Emotional Connection (EmC) process relies on understanding each member's attachment style so as to recognize his or her natural responses and protective behaviors. *Bonding conversations* are used in the process of addressing attachment problems in team interactions.[2] These conversations are intended at softening the pursuer, re-engaging the withdrawer, and helping team members to express their emotions and their fears openly. Most importantly, the conversations help them identify what is needed to feel safe and connected. Pursuers and withdrawers, while fundamentally wired in one or the other style, from time to time, adapt to the changing conditions within their working context. For example, a pursuer who feels shut out or consistently rejected may exhibit burn out and show themselves as a withdrawer. Conversely, a withdrawer who feels continuously under attack may, from time to time, exhibit pursuer characteristics by aggressively seeking connections. Without proper intervention, neither of these individuals will be successful in reconnecting.

## What Is Your Attachment Style?

What style of attachment do you prefer? Are you like us, pursuing to get things done and move forward? Or, do you avoid hassles and conflicts by withdrawing yourself from the scene, waiting till the storm passes away? Can you see your co-workers' attachment style? Do you see how conflicts spin out of control when people do not understand each other's attachment styles? It is important to note that there is no value judgment attached to a particular attachment style; it simply indicates our automatic response mechanism. Let us take a closer look at Linda's team and understand the attachment styles of the different team members.

## Meeting Linda and Her Team

As you recall from Chapter 1, Linda is experiencing conflict with her team. Her two vice presidents were not at the conference call that was important to Linda. Her response was to increase the number of meetings, which proved to be unpopular and widened the conflict. Linda leads the Western Region for Alfa Insurance Company. She manages 33 locations. Her direct reports are Vice Presidents: John, Ann, and Bob; a Division Manager, Alan; and an Executive Assistant, Evelyn. In the past six years, she has raised the bar for her team in the company and has transformed the region to be the number one in the Western United States. Upon talking with Linda on the phone, Lola noticed several cues that helped her to determine Linda's attachment style. In particular, the speed of her speech and her raised voice were the primary clues indicating a pursuer's characteristics. In addition, her complaining and judging of the situation and her solution to create additional meetings clearly confirmed Lola's assumption that Linda is a pursuer in her team relationship. This is often represented by catastrophizing, bringing in irrelevant issues into the conversation, being angry and confrontational in their response.[3]

Vice President John has been at the company longer than Linda, and he oversees 11 locations. He is an expert in his field. Although there were many challenges working with Linda in the beginning, John respects Linda's leadership guidance and implemented a lot of her suggestions. His locations have been doing quite well in the last three years. John is critical to the company and is respected by his employees. John's response to additional meetings was to freeze and say nothing, withdrawing himself from the conflict, in contrast to Linda's pursuer approach.

Vice President Ann is described as a go-getter and very involved in the community. She manages seven locations. She has been with the company for five years and has contributed significantly to the growth of her region. Linda considers Ann to be a hard worker and someone who is passionate about her work. Ann is an ambitious professional. Ann's response to the additional meetings was reported as combative and aggressive. She mentioned in the team session that she was quite troubled by Linda's decisions. Ann is a withdrawer by nature, as her usual response to stressful situations is to first disengage and then completely shut down, removing herself from the situation. But, her ambitions and the apparent safety she felt with the facilitator in the room made her respond in a pursuer manner.

Vice President Bob has been working at the company for the last seven years and loves working with Linda. Linda has been a great mentor to Bob and has helped him grow and develop as a leader. Employees love Bob as he is very personable, caring, and also ambitious. He provides his employees with tools to do their work and opportunities to shine. Bob manages 15 locations. Bob's immediate reaction—to defend and blame others—indicated to Lola that he is a pursuer in his relationship with the team.

Division Manager Alan has been working at the company for six years and does data analysis for the team. Alan does not supervise employees and mostly works closely with Linda. He provides support and reviews monthly reports that John, Ann, and Bob submit to Linda. Alan also provides training on insurance products and has a good relationship with each of his peers, and he is typically silent at meetings. In particular, in this conflict, Alan did not actively participate in the discourse. He is a withdrawer in his relationship with the team.

As an Executive Assistant, Evelyn has worked with Linda for the last four years. Evelyn and Linda are very close. Linda includes Evelyn in all of her events and meetings and takes her on trips with her. Evelyn provides some support to John, Ann, Bob, and Alan. But mostly, she is there to help Linda with whatever she needs to make her job more manageable. Evelyn is a pursuer in her relationship with the team.

All members of the team are well educated and have deep and successful experiences at other companies prior to coming to Alfa. They care a lot about Alfa's mission, and they care about their roles within the company. Lately, the team feels that Linda has become very upset with them, and whenever she voices her disappointment, she becomes aggressive and intimidating toward them. Linda deals with the situation by becoming more controlling and demanding. She starts to lecture the team, telling what needs to be done and how to act with their employees. In these situations, John, Ann, and Alan typically refrain from saying

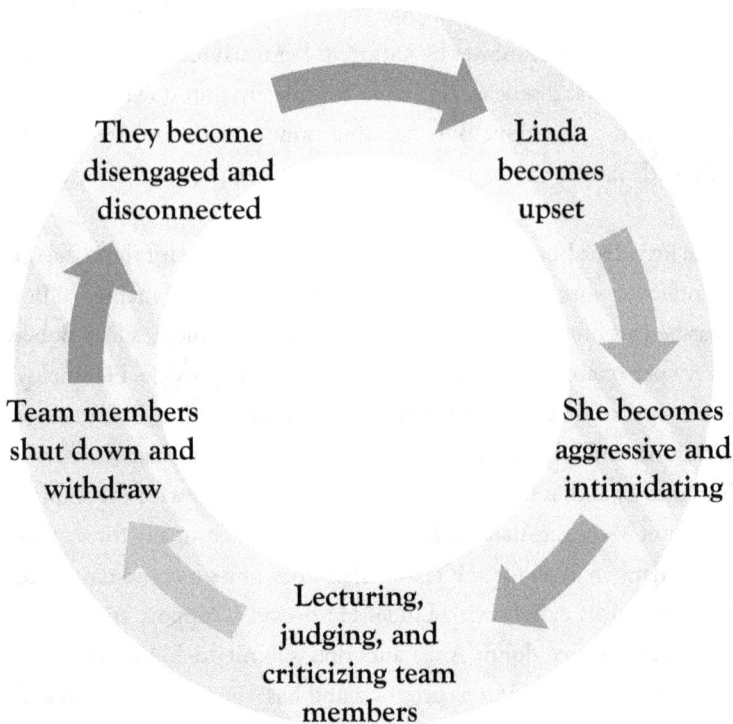

*Figure 2.1  Typical negative cycle*

anything, and the less they respond, the more aggressive Linda gets. This is their pattern. In this case, the disengagement of the withdrawers fuels the pursuer to be more demanding, thus creating a negative cycle, as shown in Figure 2.1.

## First Session With Linda and Her Team

Lola's first session was held on a sunny afternoon in a nice conference room. However, all six individuals looked very uncomfortable. Lola could feel the tension in the room, and their body language provided interesting clues. Linda paced the room. Bob was glued to his phone. Ann sat at the table with sadness on her face, looking down. John did not make any eye contact, and Evelyn appeared busy. In contrast to the others, Alan looked alert and was attentive. The first step in the EmC process is to create safety and alliance with each member of the team. Typically, in the session, Lola offers her appreciation for their attendance, acknowledges their courage, and affirms the importance of them being present. The process involves initiating team members into the realm of emotions and changing perspectives. As such, it takes a great deal of strength and courage to exhibit vulnerability in the workplace. It is essential that Lola acknowledge their presence and the degree to which they impact each other. Next, we describe the first few minutes of the first session with Linda's team.

As the facilitator, after the initial introduction and acknowledgment, Lola began the session by stating, "I understand that there has been a disconnect recently?"

Ann responded first, "Actually, the problem started two months ago."

Lola replied, "Could you help me to understand what happened two months ago?"

Ann then responded,

Linda was getting ready to go on a trip, and she asked everyone to be on a conference call, which was scheduled last minute. I had already committed that day to another meeting. I got very stressed about it. I phoned John and said that I couldn't be on the call and asked if he can report for me. Then I get a phone call from Evelyn saying that Linda is really furious with me that I didn't show up for the conference call and that Linda is changing the meetings to be weekly on Mondays. I panicked because I have weekly committee meetings at the same time. There are several people involved, so I can't change the meeting time.

Ann was clearly agitated and troubled as she recounted what had happened. The intensity of her remarks was gripping the whole room. All eyes were on Ann. It took remarkable courage for her to continue to tell me the rest of her story.

"I don't understand," Ann continued,

just because I didn't show up at the conference call, Linda is changing the meeting frequency? I work so hard, day and night, and sometimes even on weekends. I felt like Linda was punishing me and others because we missed this damn conference call.

I was pretty upset and did not feel like talking with Linda about it. I mean, I called in to apologize, but I was really, really upset, and I still feel upset about it. I mean, she showed no interest or even a concern about what was happening with me on that day. She did not even ask, and neither did Evelyn. I know that Linda generally cares, but at that moment, I felt that she didn't care about me.

Tears rolled down Ann's cheeks as she was talking.
As Linda looked at Ann, her tears started rolling down her cheeks as well. Linda jumped in and said,

Ann, I do appreciate you, I do, but you know that I've been waiting for this trip for a long time and how much it meant to me. I needed to know that everything was okay before I go on the trip. And when you didn't show up, I started to lose control, like what I was needing didn't matter, it was not important.

As a facilitator, at this point, Lola used the opportunity to slow things down in order to help participants understand their triggers and emotions. We call this the slow-motion camera technique in the EmC process.

## Understanding by Slowing Things Down

The slow-motion camera is a technical way of doing what most of us do when confronted with multiple inputs. We stop the inputs in order to understand each of them, giving us the best chance at a proper response. In the case of emotions as inputs, this task is even more crucial because emotions from others invoke emotions in us—thus complicating an already explosive situation. Slowing down the process is critical to restructuring the negative interaction.

In the EmC process, we use the slow-motion camera also to engage individuals to further clarify their particular emotions at the very moment that they are occurring. By taking the time to vocalize their thought patterns, we (the individuals and the facilitator) gain a more in-depth insight into the disconnection experienced, which is demonstrated through the conflict that is being observed. A key challenge in conflict resolution or management is the difficulty associated with the brain's preoccupation with past actions or its desire for foolproof solutions to eliminate future conflicts. Neither of these is particularly helpful as reconnection can only occur in the present. The slow-motion camera has the additional advantage of bringing everyone into the present and focusing them on how they are feeling and thinking at this very moment. That is very important because working in the present is an essential element of the EmC process. Let us take a moment to further explore what the EmC process can do and how it will help Linda and her team.

Bowlby based his research on the premise that human beings function at their best in a healthy and positive way when they are able to create close emotional connections.[4] Bowlby's definition of best is when individuals are at their creative peak, thriving, risking, open to new ideas, trusting, collaborating, and otherwise engaging life. Focusing on creating a new corrective emotional experience is how people change their behavior, according to Bowlby.

The EmC process is focused on using emotional attachment as the means to drive new and more positive emotional experiences, which, over time, lead to behavioral changes. We do not attempt behavior change, but rather we make it possible through the explorations of emotions for the individual to change their behavior over time. The EmC process is not therapeutic in nature but instead focuses on a set of processes that have shown overtime to be effective in enabling positive behavioral change. We know from attachment science that a felt sense of connection brings us emotional balance. As Bowlby noted, this balance allows us to be open to new ideas and engage with others in exploring new options. The disruption of our critical connections arouses anxiety in the pursuers and fear in the withdrawers, which becomes obvious in the conflict through blame and defense. It is important to note that situational context and roles within the organization can potentially influence an individual's attachment style: pursuer and withdrawer. That is to say that given a management role, a withdrawer may present himself or herself as a pursuer and vice versa. However, given enough time in the process, most people will settle into the style natural to them, regardless of their position or context.

In the example of Linda's team, we see this most visibly in the following interactions. In the conversation between Ann and Linda in the session, we can observe how Ann is defending her reaction by stating, "… I work so hard, day and night, and sometimes even on weekends. I felt like Linda was punishing me …" In turn, we hear Linda placing blame by the following statement, "Ann, I do appreciate you, I do, but you know that I've been waiting for this trip for a long time and how much it meant to me …"

During conflicts, despite our best intentions, we are highly prone to reactions that are based on our learned behavior when we were children. These are often best described through our immediate need to place blame on others or defend our actions. These behaviors, while generally understood in childhood, are disruptive and dysfunctional at the workplace. Unchecked and unresolved, they often morph into creating highly toxic work environments often invisible to the eye but known by the people who work there. The EmC process does not instruct individuals to stop their blame or defense, but to address the underlying emotions that are leading them toward these behaviors and eventually changing their response mechanism in a more positive direction. For example, an individual who often blames others as his or her primary response has an underlying sense of fear from past actions or has unfounded concerns. Emotions, and not the content, are the most powerful presence in the room during conflicts. They are also the most powerful agents of change. To change emotions, one needs to explore the present emotions. Often, that is where most other techniques fall short. Various approaches identify emotions, but they do not further explore and address the emotions themselves. We will dive deeper into how we explore emotions in the EmC process in the next chapter.

## Questions for Reflection

To further reflect on your own attachment style, you may wish to think through these exercise questions:

1. Write down for yourself how you respond in a situation of pressure. What is your attachment style?
2. Do you find yourself pursuing the connection or avoiding by withdrawing to preserve the connection? Do you think your style was beneficial to solving the problems you faced in the past?

3. If you envision a particular conflict, can you use the slow-motion camera and outline some of the emotions in yourself and others in the room?

## Summary of Chapter 2

In this chapter, we learned that our emotional responses are formed in our childhood, and our childlike behavior in times of stress does not serve us well in adulthood. We explored the three different attachment styles: secure, avoidant, and anxious, which are essential in how we react to conflict and determine the first set of actions. We further learned the two predominant reaction modes of withdrawer or pursuer. We met Linda's team and learned about their background and reviewed the initial conflict and used Linda and Ann to understand their responses in terms of their attachment fears. Using the slow-motion camera, we saw the opportunity to understand their reactions and responses further, which will allow us to explore the deeper emotions evoked during their disconnect.

# CHAPTER 3

# How Responses Are Shaped: The Power of Connections

To better understand connections and the power they hold in our everyday life, we begin with evaluating our emotional response at the earliest stages of our lives—when we are babies. Our brains recognize and tune in to the people whom we depend on. Edward Tronick and his team at Harvard demonstrated this phenomenon through their now-famous Still Face Experiment.[1] They found that when humans are disconnected, they go through a sequence of automatic behaviors to gain back the connection. The experiment begins with a baby and the mother in a room interacting and playing. Then, the mother is asked to act as non-responsive—to have a still face. When the baby tries to make a natural connection, the mother does not respond at all; not physically nor verbally. This creates a sequence of reactions.

First, the baby tries to attract the attention of the mother by reaching out with her hands, without sound, making eye contact, and pointing. Being unsuccessful in getting a response from the mother, the baby automatically moves into the next level of reaction. The baby starts to shriek as a signal, pushing for connection. What the baby is really trying to say is, "What happened to you? What's going on? Can't you hear me?" Being still unsuccessful as the experiment forces the mother to remain non-responsive, the baby moves to the next stage of automatic reactions. The baby turns away from the mother and shuts down. After a short period with the mother's continued non-responsiveness, the baby enters into the final stage by crying. The mother is finally permitted to respond to the baby, at which point, all is forgiven, and the baby stops crying and re-engages with the mother. The disconnection has been repaired, and the bond has been restored.

A similar sequence of actions can be observed when we view adults in professional settings where a connection has been broken. Initially, adults send signals through their facial expressions, body language, meeting behavior, or moving their chairs around—any nonverbal manner to indicate their need for attention (in the disconnection sense). Next, they turn to vocalizing their emotional state through a combination of blaming, judging, defending, lecturing, and complaining in order to bring attention to the disconnection. Whether for pursuers or withdrawers, adults in conflict will literally turn their body away or leave by withdrawing from the situation in order to preserve the connection. In essence, when we shut down and say to ourselves, "Well, I am not going to talk to you. I am not going to respond to you. I have better things to do than helping you." We shut down our own emotions to somehow change the situation, but that does not help. As the last stage, assuming the connection has not been repaired, we witness fear and panic, demonstrated through angry e-mails, all capital letters, or raised voices, resulting in responses such as yelling, screaming, crying, or stonewalling.[2] All these behaviors are a sign of desperation to reconnect.

Lola reflecting on her own experience, remembers occasions when she reached the last phase, that of feeling helpless, alone, and desperate for connection; those were painful moments that often resulted in locking herself in the office and crying. Not everybody cries, of course. Some people become angry, shout, or become extremely defensive. But underneath, they share the same feelings of fear and panic.

*Do you recognize the sequence of behavior? Have you ever experienced these feelings yourself?*

The experiment ends with the mother reaching for the baby. Her face and eyes are open, and she smiles; all of her nonverbal cues send a clear message of, "I am here." The mother becomes available, the baby responds, and the connection is repaired. There is joy again, the bonding is restored, and safety forms the foundation of their relationship once again. The EmC process seeks to enable emotional connection that has been broken in the conflict. Simply put, the process is a roadmap that allows for identifying emotions and fears, the indication of needs through sharing individual vulnerabilities, and the affirmation of those needs, which provides the opportunity for repair and reconnection. Just as with the baby, the process allows for feelings of happiness, safety, and confidence to return almost immediately upon reconnection. By giving space and words to what we feel is happening when we experience a disconnect, we allow for a path toward the restoration of the connection. Mario Mikulincer, in his series of studies, indicates that when people delve into their emotions to understand what they need to feel safe and connected, they are able to regulate their emotions and convey clearly their needs, they are able to pull people closer—responsiveness and emotional accessibility form the basis for secure bonding.[3]

## Nurturing Connection and Emotional Safety

Charles Darwin, famous for his contributions to the science of human evolution, once said, "Survival goes to the most nurtured." We also can see the same phenomena in the dynamics of team behavior.

As a team leader, keeping healthy connections between team members makes them feel emotionally safe. This feeling of safety is critical to their ability to form secure bonds, engage in creative work, and trust each other, especially during times of difficulty and uncertainty. We do this by first helping team members become aware of their own emotions and reactions to stress.

Why focus on emotions? Because our emotions tell us what matters and orient us in the proper direction. Emotions steer us to what is worthwhile and away from danger. They are our survival compass. In our work with teams and organizational leaders, we find that emotions in business settings are often dismissed or, at best, given little attention. The workplace emphasizes the habit of separating emotions from cognition when making decisions and analyzing problems; we often use the language of logical or dispassionate analyses, ignoring the emotional component. But, in research and practice, this approach proves to be a mistake because emotion and cognition have to work together for us to respond appropriately to complex and challenging situations. As with the case of the baby, if there is continued or repeated disconnection that does not provide the baby the validation for safety, over time, the baby develops set reactions that carry into adulthood. These reactions in adults are often verbalized, such as: feeling abandoned, not being seen as good enough, not feeling acknowledged or valued, feeling judged, or demeaned. These feelings, when formed, become part of us and, at times of stress or conflict, are triggered.

In the EmC process, we refer to these as raw spots, experiences from the past that become painful again in a similar situation. Some triggers could be a raised tone of voice, a disapproving or angry facial expression, particular words, and behaviors. The triggers create an instant disconnect based on our raw spots. For example, being left out of an e-mail could be interpreted as being deliberately excluded—triggering feelings of exclusion or of not being valued—whereas it may have simply been a mistake. The raw spots for the individual emerge out of the experiences where he or she may have been left out of decisions or information in the past. Studies show that in attachment relationships, in only 100 milliseconds, we are able to read facial expressions, and in 300 milliseconds, we are able to feel what we see on the other person's face.[4] In essence, we can pick up facial cues almost instantaneously. Negative facial expressions can trigger immediate panic as functional magnetic resonance imaging (fMRI)[5] studies of the brain show the facial expressions of rejection are processed in the same area of the brain as physical pain. Thus, in a manner of speaking, seeing a rejection on your boss's face is the same as stepping on a nail.[6] Other triggers may include unusual and surprising decisions, disproportionate actions, or obvious disengagement.

We have all experienced moments of disconnection at work and can relate to how painful they are. The inability to reconnect or the lack of knowledge about how to reconnect and to heal these painful moments creates additional raw spots that can be triggered whenever we are confronted in moments of stress or crisis. Raw spots can also occur when our emotions or needs are dismissed or ignored. The failure to address our needs, in a sense, scrapes our emotional skin raw and creates a relationship injury. Although our natural response is to keep our distance or become aggressive toward others when hurt, this behavior does not heal our raw spots and only makes matters worse. From our experience, the only way to reduce the impact of the raw spots on our reactions is through bonding conversations, which lead to reconnection.

## Identifying the Triggers

The first step in healing a relationship injury is to identify the triggers. Let us look at Linda and her team to see what were some of the triggers during the conflict:

- *For Linda: Ann and Bob's absence during the conference call*
- *For Ann: Linda's decision of changing the calls to be every Monday morning*
- *For John: Linda's action of interrupting and canceling the conference call*
- *For Bob: Evelyn's words that Linda was furious*
- *For Alan and Evelyn: Linda's raised voice and her facial expression of looking angry*

As we can see, people at work impact each other in numerous ways. They react to inputs during a moment of stress from the vantage point of their perception of the individual or individuals with whom they seek attachment. Triggers can be minute actions that, at times, are invisible or inconsequential to someone else. However, they carry loud messages to the person being triggered. It is important to recognize that it takes courage for individuals to share their triggers and raw spots. The EmC process is oriented toward creating emotional safety so that such sharing can take place. The individual can then reframe the conflict in terms of the negative cycle that is feeding the conflict and taking over the relationship. This reframing removes the blame away from the individuals and aligns them against the cycle, not each other. This critical focus on the negative cycle helps team members feel united and less threatened, thus increasing their willingness to continue the process and positively engage each other.

In the EmC process, we provide a list of 16 separate raw spots and three levels of emotions, so that team members have an extensive language to express their experience properly. A full list of raw spots is included in Appendix A. Here are a few examples of the raw spots for the various members of Linda's team:

- *Linda's raw spots were not being valued or appreciated for her work and communicating her needs, but being ignored.*

- *Ann's raw spots were not being valued or appreciated for her work and being judged as not good enough.*
- *John's raw spots were not being valued or appreciated for his time when someone turns away from him by canceling the conference call right in front of him. He felt that someone close to him was telling him that he did not deserve Linda's time to hear his report.*
- *Bob's raw spots were being judged as not good enough. Just because the call was not on his calendar, he did not deserve respect or consideration to be informed. He was being judged for something that he did not even know that he had missed.*
- *Alan and Evelyn both felt the same raw spot of someone close to them is being aggressive or intimidating toward them.*

As the facilitator, Lola observed changes to the face and body posture of each of the team members as they shared their raw spots and triggers. The EmC process helps to maintain a level of safety for each individual as they share emotional experiences (raw spots, triggers, and emotions). We do this for each person before turning to the next individual. Doing so provides the space for each person to be heard, validated, and reassured—at which point, we often observe team members becoming calmer and more reflective. After we have identified triggers and raw spots, we then explore emotions, which we will cover in the next chapter.

## Questions for Reflection

Here are some questions for you to use to reflect on the key concepts in this chapter:

1. In thinking through a conflict or a relationship crisis, can you name some of the actions or words which were triggers for you?
2. In relation to these triggers, can you outline some of the raw spots that were touched?
3. How did the triggers and the raw spots impact your interaction with the other individual(s)?
4. Can you observe when others get triggered by something you said or did?

5. Can you follow through to observe which raw spots may have been touched in them?

## Summary of Chapter 3

In this chapter, we began with the review of the Still Face Experiment with the baby and the mother, which illustrates the four levels of response: reaching, pushing, withdrawing, and overwhelming panic. We discussed how these responses carry forward to adulthood and form the basis of our reactions in moments of disconnect with those whom we seek attachment. We discussed the importance of recognizing emotions in the workplace and the role they play in our ability to form secure bonds or to find ourselves amidst periods of disconnect. While the content and our objective goals and aspirations are critical in business, the role of emotions has been generally downplayed, leading to disconnections and ineffective workplace behaviors. We learned through various studies that rejection from or disconnection with individuals who are important in our life, be they at work or at home, is painful. In fact, fMRI studies show that the pain of rejection is processed in the same area of the brain as physical pain. We are hurt when we lose connections. The inability or the lack of willingness to properly address the depth of the emotions, the pain of rejection, and the nature of the disconnection occurs regularly in many workplaces. As was the case with the baby, the adults at work react improperly by protesting the continued disconnection. The perpetual negative cycle that is created and fed through ineffective strategies to reconnect causes further conflicts.

A primary goal of the EmC process is to uncover the underlying key triggers and raw spots that have resulted in the formation and continuous feeding of the negative cycles experienced by those in conflict. The EmC process provides extensive language and situational safety to help individuals properly distinguish and share their raw spots and triggers. This allows for a shared understanding of the negative cycle as the primary opponent in the battle to gain reconnection—thus removing the burden of blame or defense from individuals so that a path forward can be explored.

# CHAPTER 4

# Exploring Emotions

*Chapters 4, 5, 6, and 7 explore in depth the various components of emotional connection and the process through which relationship bonds are formed, repaired, and nurtured. These chapters contain detailed information requiring careful reading and analysis.*

We distinguish three levels of emotions in the EmC process: surface emotions, softer emotions, and primary emotions. Exploring each level of emotion takes us deeper into understanding the core reactions and protective behaviors that impact our interactions with others during moments of stress. The iceberg in Figure 4.1 illustrates the dangers of not discovering and engaging our emotions beneath the surface. These deeper emotions are responsible for sinking our efforts at resolving conflicts.

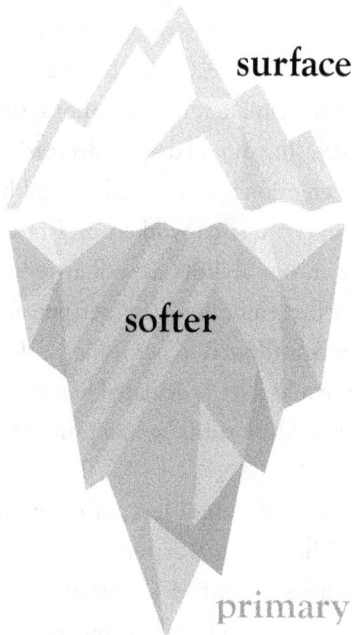

surface

softer

primary

Figure 4.1 The emotional iceberg

Let us discuss the three levels of emotions in more detail.

## Surface, Softer, and Primary Emotions

*Surface emotions* form the first level of our emotions when we are stressed. Surface emotions are those that are visible to us. They are easy to identify: they are on the surface. We often label them as the emotions of feeling frustrated, annoyed, disappointed, betrayed, angry, confused, tense, and so on (see Appendix B for a full list). All in all, we have distinguished 15 separate surface emotions. Unchecked surface emotions create a significant imbalance that can quickly escalate into actions, which may be difficult to reverse. For example, Linda's anger led her to make an immediate decision to increase the frequency of her meetings, which, of course, snowballed into a full conflict. By the sheer articulation of surface emotions, Linda could have given herself a chance to examine various options before acting.

*Softer emotions* are beneath the surface. These are more vulnerable emotions and much harder to see. Most people find it difficult to share softer emotions, especially in the workplace setting. We have distinguished 21 separate softer emotions. As an example, they are feeling embarrassed, intimidated, overwhelmed, helpless, rejected, abandoned, and so on (see Appendix B for a full list). Unlike surface emotions, softer emotions weigh us down by either increasing our anxiety or decreasing our willingness to move forward. Softer emotions carry the additional burden of increasing the chance of rejection by our co-workers and bosses. These emotions shake our confidence in our abilities as well as reduce trust at work. In our example, Ann's softer emotions were her perceived inadequacies in her abilities, and they contributed to her feeling defeated. By sharing her softer emotions, Ann could have articulated her sense of inadequacy and defeat, which Linda would, in turn, be in a position to respond to more positively.

*Primary emotions* form the third level of emotions, which are at the heart of the matter. They are the driver for much of our actions and reactions. Scientists have identified six primary emotions: fear, sadness, shame, surprise, anger, and joy.[1] In our experience, fear accounts for over 60 percent of the root cause of most conflicts. Fear is the most powerful of the primary emotions because it is essentially about safety and multi-dimensional in its effect. Our whole nervous system is obsessed with threats. When we feel fear, our rational response and logical understanding of situations stop. Fear comes first. It takes control by focusing our brain on getting us to safety. Relationships and connections are essential to our emotional existence. When we get disconnected, our brain interprets the disconnect as a danger cue, which places fear firmly in the driver seat. Fear knocks us off-balance and makes the processing of other information very difficult. It has physical manifestations that are felt throughout our body, often resulting in tightening of the chest, pain in the shoulders, and pins-and-needles throughout the body. Our eyes become focused and get smaller, the muscles tighten, and the heart starts beating faster. Fear limits our ability to engage and collaborate our openness to ideas, and connection with our work partners.[2]

Feelings of abandonment or rejection are often rooted in sadness. Sadness results in feeling stuck, helpless, and hopeless at times, disabling the individual from taking action. Sadness at work, while disarming and capable of bringing about empathy, eventually serves to disconnect the individual from the community. This further alienates the individual by deepening the emotional hole, thereby enforcing the person's inaction. Individuals with depression often cite their sadness as their inability to take positive actions during challenging times.

Shame is an emotion that leads to hiding, avoiding, and feeling inadequate. It is often felt in the stomach and is reported by many as a feeling of extreme discomfort. Shame prevents us from properly evaluating the role of various individuals within a conflict by unduly focusing on our shortcomings. In addition to the actions of avoiding and hiding, shame drives us further into disconnection from projects and commitments in the workplace, isolating us from our professional relationships. Moreover, shame permeates our personal lives outside of work to a greater degree than the other primary emotions because it is rooted in our perception of having done something wrong. Shame is damaging to our psyche and traumatizes beyond the other emotions preventing personal and professional growth.

As a primary emotion, surprise carries a positive outcome when connections are secure; it helps us be attentive and explore opportunities. However, when the connection is insecure, surprise manifests itself as fear or shame, which creates distrust and suspicion. In dysfunctional work environments, surprise leads to significant anxiety and discord, as the organization is forced to face weaknesses in connections within team members. Surprise, even in the best of circumstances, has the propensity to generate feelings of exclusion, which is interpreted automatically by our mammalian brain as a danger cue. We need regularity and clarity in order to stay balanced. Surprise throws us off of that balance.

Anger is about the need to assert and defend the self. Anger is a powerful emotion that creates a great deal of fear in the workplace. Feeling angry is exhausting. While some classify anger as a primary emotion, in our experience, we find anger serving as a surface emotion, with fear acting as the underlying emotion. Anger causes considerable trauma by terrifying people in the workplace, freezing progress, and blocking creativity. Anger directly and quickly can create a feeling of shame and inadequacy in the workplace, which will take considerable energy to undo.

Joy is about contact and engagement. The feeling of joy makes us stronger and confident, becoming more resilient to stress. It allows us to remain engaged and be less likely to get anxious or depressed. Collaboration and support of others increases as people report a feeling of joy at work. Research shows those team members who feel joy become more effective through greater motivation and creativity, which we all know leads to better business results.[3]

The EmC process is focused on helping team members move from negative emotions we discussed earlier into the feeling of joy—where they can grow and thrive professionally and personally. Knowing these three layers of emotions, we expand the emotional terrain by providing team members with the ability and the language to be articulate in expressing how they feel. Moreover, the process creates the opportunity to also understand and be more in tune with other people's feelings—all of which will reduce the overwhelming sensation in a moment of change.

## Understanding Emotions Is Not Enough

As emotions are intimidating, understanding them must be followed by knowing how to work with them. The first step in working with emotions is knowing how to respond in a way that creates safety.

Here are some important questions for you to consider:

- *How do you respond to emotions with others?*
- *When you see others struggle emotionally, do you have an urge to fix the situation?*
- *When others share emotions, do you have an urge to dismiss or ignore their emotions?*

Typically, people feel uncomfortable in sharing emotions because they are afraid others may perceive them as weak or sharing may prove to be overwhelming to the other person. We are not used to this way of communicating with each other, but we can learn to express our emotions, have others validate them, and collectively arrive at a better understanding. It is crucial to acknowledge all emotions being expressed in order to create safety. When individuals feel safe and heard, there can be change, connection, and bonding.

Acknowledgment is the first step in managing emotions. We do this by affirming and validating the person's feelings and encouraging them to share their experience. In the EmC process, we use the following six statements for acknowledging, affirming, and validating emotions:

1. *I hear you.*
2. *I can see that this was really difficult for you.*
3. *This can be very stressful.*
4. *Your feelings are valid.*
5. *I feel very honored that you would share this with me.*
6. *I can see how much this matters to you.*

Practicing these phrases will greatly help in delivering them in an authentic and non-scripted way. In addition, ensuring a calm and relaxed composure during the time when someone is expressing their emotions will allow them to continue to use the opportunity to go deeper into the layers we discussed earlier. As we use this language, we feel closer to our team members, creating a new emotional experience that will help us be connected.

## Exploring Emotions With Linda's Team

Using the slow-motion camera and properly responding to the emotions being discussed, Lola created safety with Linda's team for individuals to share their feelings and thoughts. She learned the following:

John felt angry and rejected because he had prepared for the meeting, and Linda's abrupt cancellation resulted in him feeling ignored and dismissed.

In his own words, he said, "I felt like a cloud came over me. I was on the call and ready to do my report when Linda abruptly interrupted me and said, 'Where are Ann and Bob? Why are they not on the call?' I said, 'I don't know. Can I continue?' But Linda said, 'Hold on.' Then she puts me on hold, and after a few minutes, she says, 'We are going to cancel the call because Ann and Bob are not on the call.' Well, I was on the call, Alan and Evelyn were on the call. I felt like, why is she canceling the call just because Ann and Bob didn't show up? I felt completely ignored and dismissed. I don't think I said one word afterward."

John continued telling Lola his story, "Once Linda makes up her mind, she becomes like a sergeant giving orders, and at that point, I start to move away, like fog covers me, and I just can't hear anything of what she is saying. I felt rejected as if my work was not important to Linda. I remember thinking to myself, what am I doing here? Why am I trying so hard? Is this not important enough for Linda to take the time and listen to what I have to say? Somehow, the only place I felt safe was to close down and shut her out."

Bob, who had missed this meeting, felt confused and panicked. In his own words, he said, "I am sitting here and thinking, why did I miss this meeting? The meeting is not even on my calendar. I had some interviews scheduled that day, but I did not get the meeting invitation. And if it was so important to Linda, why didn't Evelyn remind us a day before? I mean, how can we prevent this from happening in the future?"

Alan felt shut down during the initial meeting response but felt happy in the EmC session because we were addressing the bigger problems in their communication. In his own words, he said, "I'm actually grateful that this is coming out because we get into these miscommunications, and then we never talk about it. So, I'm grateful."

Evelyn felt scared and panicked. She said, "Well, I was really scared, and I could hear my heart beating faster, and then I look at Linda, and she was really furious. And when she gets furious, you better watch out. It's like a hurricane is coming. I thought to myself, Oh, shoot! Ann and Bob are in trouble. I'm getting further and further away from Linda."

As a facilitator, Lola used this opportunity to slow things down through the slow-motion camera to further understand and explore the underlying emotions and thoughts. The following is a dialogue between Lola as a facilitator and, in this case, Evelyn, to illustrate the slow-motion camera and continuous use of affirming language:

| Facilitator: | Yes, the connection between you and Linda is getting further away? She's getting angry, she is furious, she is no longer moving with you. |
|---|---|
| Evelyn: | Yes, yes. And every minute she's becoming angrier, the further and further away I get. |
| Facilitator: | And what do you do then? |
| Evelyn: | I start to panic. I shiver inside. I'm terrified and filled with fear. |
| Facilitator: | Yes. You're saying I'm filled with fear. I'm terrified, and I start to panic. |
| Evelyn: | Yes, I don't want to be afraid, I love Linda and love working with her, but at that moment, I become terrified. |
| Facilitator: | And what do you see as you become terrified? |
| Evelyn: | I see this caring person suddenly turn into a frightening, large person who is above me, roaring at the top of her lungs. |
| Facilitator: | And the bigger this person gets, what happens to you? |
| Evelyn: | The more I shiver, the smaller I get. |
| Facilitator: | Yes. |
| Evelyn: | And, the more scared I get, the smaller I become. |

As you can see, by slowing down the emotional responses, we were able to learn more from Evelyn about the emotions she was feeling during the disconnect. At the same time, we were able to use the slow-motion camera to cool down the situation. It is clear that Linda has lost the connection with her team, leaving them feeling rejected and abandoned. Ironically, Linda's own reaction is also that of being rejected and abandoned. With all the desire to connect, Linda ended up pushing her team away by becoming furious and scary in her response. The team became more withdrawn and disconnected, which in turn made Linda, who is a pursuer by nature, even more desperate for connection. That is the cycle: Linda pushes, her team withdraws. The more the team withdraws, the more Linda pushes, and they are caught in a terrible negative cycle, a dance where they are not able to dance together (See Figure 2.1, pg. 16.).

## Revealing the Details

Let us examine how the EmC process reveals the emotional details of the various disconnects. Part of working with conflict is to know how to work with withdrawers and pursuers. We now know that for withdrawers, shutting down is an active effort; suppressing emotions is a hard task, as it takes energy for the brain, and it is challenging to sustain it for too long. The goal is to help withdrawers feel a sense of safety and for their minds to relax in order to re-engage and allow them to be present in the conversation.

For pursuers, on the other hand, our goal is to soften their approach and acknowledge their feelings so that they feel that they have been heard. As pursuers actively pursue to reconnect, they become exhausted from being disheartened by the withdrawers' disengagement. By helping them feel heard, they begin to share their emotions in a calmer and more focused manner, thus creating a better environment for withdrawers to remain in the conversation. In the situation with Linda and her team, it became evident that the disconnect had very little to do with the incident around the meeting. The emotions that came up during the session had deeper roots than what was visible on the surface. Each person in this team was triggered by the incident in different ways and responded based on their past experiences and their immediate sense of connection with Linda.

## The Three Layers of Emotions in Linda's Team

Let us look at the three layers of emotions for Linda and Ann as an example:

Linda felt frustrated, upset, and angry. Her softer emotions were feeling dismissed, being let down, feeling helpless, hurt, failing, abandoned, not valued, and not important. She felt fear and sadness as her primary emotions.

Ann felt frustrated, irritated, frozen, upset, tense, confused, and alone. For the softer emotions, she felt worried, isolated, helpless, hopeless, hurt, panicked, intimidated, rejected, abandoned, defeated, not heard, and not valued. And, her primary emotions were feeling surprised and sad.

### Can you see the difference between Ann and Linda's experiences?

When we hear the tumult of emotions each person was feeling, it is easy to see how each got caught in a negative cycle. Also, it was interesting that underneath their emotions, they all felt sad for the loss of connection with each other. This shows how important they are to each other. As each person shared their emotions, the energy in the room shifted from stiff and hot to relaxed and warm; Lola saw each person take a sigh of relief.

## How Can Emotions Be Captured

Magda B. Arnold was the first contemporary theorist to develop the appraisal theory of emotions.[4] In her theory, Arnold described how imaging is an essential element in processing emotions. In the EmC process, after we have identified surface, softer, and primary emotions, we ask each person to describe an image of what they experienced during the disconnect. This helps people visualize their experience, helping them and others see the dimensions of their emotions.

Linda's team shared with Lola the following powerful images:

- Linda: I was on a boat all by myself
- Ann: A rug was pulled away from under my feet
- John: A dark cloud came over me
- Bob: I was sitting in a rocking chair, watching chaos happen

- Alan: I was a deer caught in the headlight—just frozen
- Evelyn: A furious dragon appeared in front of me

## Bodily Sensations

Emotions are fast, and emotions are contagious. They have a response repertoire tied into them. We can sense these responses when we can tune into our bodily sensations. Tightness in the chest is often a reflection of fear, pain in the shoulders and neck suggests sadness, and pain felt in the stomach reflects shame. Because these feelings are quite automatic and generally not susceptible to cognitive input, they serve as a check to ensure we are correctly identifying the primary emotions.

## How Fear Highjacks Our Actions

As fear can be terrifying and is the predominant primary emotion in situations of conflict, stress, and uncertainty, the EmC process helps to clarify fear in three dimensions of attachment:

- *The fear about oneself at that moment*
- *The fear about the other person as it pertains to oneself*
- *The fear about the relationship*

If a person is busy regulating their fear, they have no room for empathy for someone else. Once we help the person articulate the fear and break it down into pieces, that generates the capacity to understand and empathize with the hurt of the other person. When team members are able to share their fears openly, they allow others to be with them in their fear and create an opportunity for a bonding moment.

Here are a few examples of Linda's team as they shared their fears:

In response to the first question about fear about themselves, the responses ranged from feeling ineffective (Linda), to losing their jobs (Ann and Evelyn), to failing (Bob), to feeling unimportant (John), and being alone (Alan). The fears about the other person(s) illustrated a similar pattern of variations, everything from lack of care to loss of support, to feeling unheard, to being seen as irresponsible. Not surprisingly, their worst fears about the relationship were generally the same, that their relationship would fall apart.

## How Can I Work With Emotions in Myself?

Recognizing emotions in ourselves is considerably harder than helping others to recognize their emotions. As emotions come fast during a moment of stress, it is hard to slow down our feelings when we are emotionally overwhelmed. During a time of strong emotion, our prefrontal cortex (the cognition part of the brain) is not in service. Instead, the mammalian brain (the amygdala) is fully in charge. During these times, it is difficult to cognitively understand what is happening. Fortunately, our brain holds on to emotionally charged experiences, and by practicing the skill of *unpacking* (slowing down and identifying) emotions, we can become more aware of the emotions we experienced during the stressful moment.

Lola recalls an incident where her emotions were unexpectedly triggered. "Someone was helping me with a password. As I was typing the letters, the person next to me said, 'Capital L!' The way that was said triggered me. I raised my hands in the air and said, 'OK!' with a raised voice, and I walked away. I did not expect to react that way! After the incident, once I had calmed down, I began to identify what had happened to me."

First, she tuned into what was happening with her bodily sensations. "Was my heart racing? Was I getting hot? Was I feeling needles in my body? Was there a tightness in my chest or pain in my stomach?" Bodily sensations provided her with the first sign that something was happening emotionally; "my environment did not feel safe." Tuning into her body opened the pathway to understand the layers of emotions such as feeling frustrated, annoyed, irritated, and tense as her surface emotions. Thinking further about the softer emotions, she felt intimidated, overwhelmed, and embarrassed. Finally, the primary emotion driving her reaction was shame. Learning this information, she felt calmer and clearer about the sequence of emotional cascades she experienced, which proved to be useful in responding to similar situations in the future.

While we cannot control all of our reactions immediately in a situation, understanding ourselves and practicing goes a long way to preventing prolonged negative cycles and more hurt feelings.

## Questions for Reflection

Here are some questions to think about, and reflect on the key concepts in this chapter:

1. Imagine a situation of conflict in the recent past. List the three layers of emotions you felt at the moment (See Appendix B).
2. In the preceding situation, can you list the emotions of others in the conflict?
3. Do you see yourself as a pursuer or withdrawer in that situation, and how did that impact your reaction?
4. Thinking about the six responses to emotions mentioned in this chapter, which ones resonate with you? How do they calm you down?
5. Can you think of the right response for some of the other people in the conflict?

## Summary of Chapter 4

In this chapter, we went deeper into the EmC process by exploring the three levels of emotions: surface, softer, and primary emotions present in any conflict or disconnection. We discussed in depth the six primary emotions of fear, sadness, shame, surprise, anger, and joy, with a deep dive into fear as the principal emotion invoked in situations of stress and emotional disconnect.

As the EmC process is focused on identifying and listing these emotions, we also discussed the six responses that are most often successful in de-escalating the crisis and providing a safe space for all participants to share their emotions and engage in productive resolution of the conflict.

We used Linda's team to list in detail each member's particular emotional response to the incident, from the EmC perspective and in each person's own words. Understanding, identifying, and processing emotions are critical steps in restructuring and reframing negative interactions.

# CHAPTER 5

# From Being Stuck to Moving On

In the previous chapters, we discussed elements of triggers, raw spots, and emotions. We will now turn to the process of interaction, and by doing so, it will help you gain a deeper understanding of the negative cycles that are responsible for conflicts and disconnections. We often believe we can steer our thoughts. But, most of the time, in times of stress, it is our emotions that are in control of our thoughts—and consequently of our actions. That is why we call them *automatic* thoughts and behaviors. They also protect us from the fears that accompany disconnections. Losing the connection with our team members triggers an alarm in the amygdala, a part of our brain that is responsible for our survival—we respond with automatic protective actions. In these moments, we do not think; instead, we feel, and then we act.[1]

Automatic thoughts drive our protective behaviors, which in situations of conflict and disconnect can start and maintain a negative cycle of interaction. When we feel disconnected, and we do not know how to slow things down, we become overwhelmed by emotions—which, taken together, neuroscientists call a *primal panic*.[2] In that moment of panic, we do one of two things: we either pursue the connection by demanding, lecturing, blaming, criticizing, and judging (seeking the connection) or withdraw by shutting down, numbing, distancing, avoiding, and stonewalling (thus preserving the connection). The protective behaviors occur unconsciously and automatically as a response to stress, but as team members continue to use their individual strategies, the terrible negative cycle pushes the team members more and more apart. As a result, they feel less safe, become more defensive, and begin to think of the other person as their enemy. This is accompanied by changes in the body language, the tone of voice, and facial expressions, further distancing individuals and feeding the negative cycle.

In the EmC process, we help team members become more aware of their automatic thoughts and protective behaviors by making them more explicit, recognizing we all have them. For pursuers, the automatic thought may sound like this: "I have to stop you. How dare you?" For withdrawers, the automatic thought could be: "I have to get away. I give up. I don't need you anyway."

In Linda's team example, their automatic thoughts were:

- *Linda: How dare you?*
- *Ann and Bob: I have to stop you.*
- *John: I give up.*
- *Alan and Evelyn: I have to get away.*

These automatic thoughts shift team members out of their emotional balance, which is often followed by protective (disruptive) behaviors that widen the distance in the relationship. For Linda's team, their protective behaviors were:

- *Linda: demand, judge, lecture, speak more quickly*
- *John: withdraw and distance*
- *Ann: distance, withdraw, and avoid*
- *Bob: defend, demand, and complain*
- *Alan and Evelyn: shut down and avoid*

Linda's team illustrates the multiple sets of automatic thoughts and protective behaviors that can exist within any team at a moment of conflict. Linda's strategy to require weekly meetings with her team exacerbated the negative cycle. It gave Ann the message that she, Ann, is not important, whereas the opposite was true. In fact, Ann is so important to Linda that when Ann did not show up for the conference call, Linda panicked.

Through the EmC process, Linda was able to share how panicked she felt, given her desperation, and gained the awareness of the impact her actions had on her team. When Ann and the rest of the team were able to hear and see Linda's emotional experience, they were able to respond to Linda and reassure her from a position of care. Linda was moved by their reassurance, feeling supported by her team at that moment. Because introspection and understanding emotions are critical to the reconnection process, the team leader should reflect, validate, and normalize each person's experience, as they are being shared, striving to stay away from language that dismisses or demeans any of the emotions team members share during the session.

Alliance and safety are always the priority in EmC, so it is very important that the team leader validate each person's viewpoint. Alliance should not be mistaken for agreement, but rather it is the validation and the acceptance of the disconnection that people experience during the conflict. Even if by all evidence, and from the content point of view, an individual overdramatizes or misinterprets things in their assessment, the EmC process is predicated in establishing an empathic understanding by creating a level playing field.

The validation component of the EmC process is critical to encouraging disclosure of underlying emotions, automatic thoughts, and protective behaviors. Doing so, we are enlightened as to the attachment cues that form the relationship between team members. These moments of vulnerability are paramount to the overall process of reconnection; they move the team toward creating a new experience. Through this experience, they can begin to reconnect and repair the bond. It is through new corrective emotional experiences that the change occurs, and behaviors are modified.[3]

## Negative Cycles—Deep Dive

What we have experienced in the previous chapters begins with an incident that initiates a sequence of events we referred to as the negative cycle. The reactions to the initial incident further exacerbate the negative cycle, although the people involved in the conflict are completely unaware of what is actually happening and why. Figure 5.1 illustrates a typical negative cycle:

Here is how the cycle goes: Person A is triggered, which in turn, touches their raw spots generating surface emotions, such as frustration, disappointment, and anger. As the individual is unable to slow things down, automatic thoughts and protective behaviors dominate the Person's A actions. As a result Person's A actions trigger Person B and their raw spots, generating surface emotions, automatic thoughts, and protective

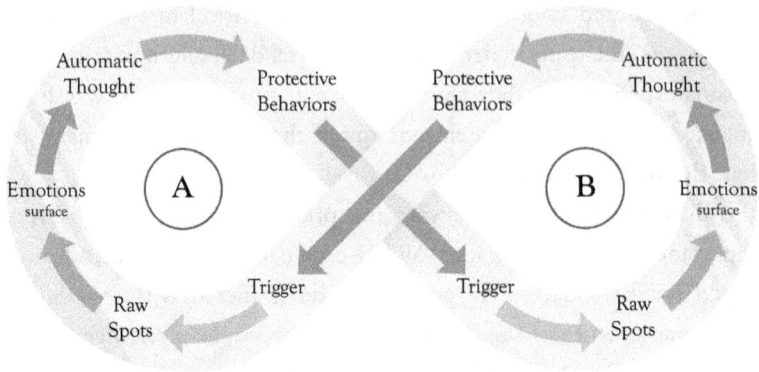

*Figure 5.1 A perpetual negative cycle of conflict*

behaviors in Person B—which in-turn trigger Person A again. This is how an infinite loop of negative cycles begins. Researchers have found several negative cycle patterns, which repeatedly occur in relation to conflicts and in times of stress.[4] These cycles have many different names. In the EmC process, we refer to them as: *attack–withdraw*, *attack–attack*, and *withdraw–withdraw*.

## The *Attack–Withdraw* Cycle

The most common negative cycle, attack–withdraw, begins with one person complaining, blaming, or criticizing, and the other person defending, distancing, and stonewalling, one pushing and the other withdrawing. The more one pushes, the more the other withdraws; the more the other withdraws, the more the other pushes; thus, a terrible negative cycle starts to take shape. These negative cycles shift the emotional balance and keep people in distress.[5] You might recognize this cycle in your environment, as it often sounds something like this (in an angry voice): "You don't respond to me. How can we work together if you don't respond to me? I keep sending you e-mail after e-mail, and I get no response. Are you ignoring me? Why don't you ever answer me?" And the other person says, "Is that right? Who can talk to someone who is angry all the time? Have you noticed that you are angry all the time? I wish you would just stop bothering me and leave me alone."

Angry criticism often triggers stonewalling, which, in turn, triggers further distancing—feeding an infinite loop of negative cycles. Withdrawers withdraw because they feel overwhelmed and do not know how to express what they want to say; they shut down in order to preserve the connection. However, what they do not realize is that when they withdraw, they shut people out—which, in contrast to what they think, makes pursuers more anxious and upset. People who pursue (the perceived attackers) feel desperate and alone; they want their connection back, but they do not realize that their aggressive pursuing works negatively by making withdrawers feel more intimidated and overwhelmed. In an extended attack–withdraw situation, the withdrawer can become overly aggressive as a result of continuous attack. Their reaction may be disproportionate and even intimidating to others. It is important to recognize that this situation has gone on too long and must be addressed immediately. At this point, the negative cycle has taken control of the relationship with each person beginning to think of the other as a threat, and they start to respond to each other, physiologically and emotionally, as if they are each in peril. Avoiding eye contact, speaking angrily, and displaying frustration and annoyance are the telltale signs of people deep in the negative cycle.

## The *Attack–Attack* Cycle

Another pattern of negative cycles is the attack–attack cycle or *find the bad guy*, as it is referred to by some researchers. In this pattern, both parties blame each other as the instigator of their conflict. In such a cycle, surface emotions run high, the atmosphere is charged, and blaming and defending are the predominant modes of interaction; individuals are incapable of hearing each other. Moreover, they appear unable to acknowledge their own emotions, which are most likely that of feelings of fear, shame, and sadness.

While the attack–attack cycle appears as war or a storm at work, it is more akin to a bad dance—where individuals are forced to participate by the requirements of position and obligation. In this cycle, the dancers are on the dance floor. However, each is dancing to a different tune and insists that their individual tune is the correct one. In the negative cycle, they step on each other's toes, blaming each other for not understanding the music or the right movements. Their conflict is undeniably loud and ultimately destructive to the team and the organization. Given that in the attack–attack cycle, both parties are on the *dance floor*, this interactional pattern is the easiest to attempt to change since individuals are actively engaged.

## The *Withdraw–Withdraw* Cycle

The withdraw–withdraw cycle, or *freeze and flee*, leaves people numb and distant.[6] In this cycle, no one seems to be on the dance floor, and they are not emotionally invested in the dance. In addition, the withdraw–withdraw cycle gives the false impression of peace and general harmony. As most managers and organizations are averse to conflict, the lack of visible conflict, in the withdraw–withdraw cycle often goes unrecognized and unresolved. Furthermore, the overall productivity and innovative capacity of the organization is severely compromised because people are not engaging and collaborating with each other.[7]

In Linda's team, we noticed two primary negative cycles in the conflicts that arose from the primary trigger, the ill-timed last-minute conference call. Given that Linda is a pursuer, we certainly saw the attack–withdraw cycle emerge between Linda and Ann, Linda and John, and Linda and Alan. Due to the strong storm of their interaction, Ann (being a withdrawer) engaged in the attack–withdraw cycle with Linda.

## How the Negative Cycle Takes Over

In general, even though the negative cycle can be obvious at times, it is important to understand how the cycle takes over our interactions. In practice, we have come across numerous examples of teams and individuals that see the cycles that are generated by their behavior, and they wish for a different mode of interaction. However, the emotions and their perceptions continue to enforce the cycle that perpetuates making the separation wider.

Fundamentally, the negative cycle is the continuous manifestation of the pain of abandonment and rejection in moments of vulnerability further reinforced when we communicate our needs into what we perceive as the black hole—no response from the other. As we feel judged or devalued, we cry out for validation and receive none or, at worse, the opposite. The impediment that prevents us from sending a clear message of connection is the very obstacle that needs to be worked through in the EmC process where we access, clarify, and engage each person's underlying emotions, fears, and attachment needs.

It is equally important to understand the *content/context* and not entirely devalue its impact on the negative cycle. The ever-changing nature of organizational priorities and modalities has a continuous impact on the many negative cycles among teams and individuals. While we realize by this point that the emotional underpinnings of the connection or the disconnections drive the behaviors, we must also be attuned to the particular context that can be modified or understood in the process of improving and eventually eliminating the negative cycles.

The EmC process allows for a corrective emotional experience that elicits and engages emotions and needs in a new context of emotional accessibility, responsiveness, and engagement, which each person ultimately seeks. Also, feeding the negative cycle are a great many preconceived notions of value (of ourselves and others), organizational hierarchy, and criticality to the mission. For example, an employee and a boss whose conflict is embedded in their inability to be vulnerable and share their painful moment are further exacerbated by the boss's preconceived hierarchical beliefs, such as "He (subordinate) needs to respect me (boss)." The EmC process, through its methodical and careful approach, attempts to remove as much as possible the content, the hierarchy, and preconceived notions in order to focus on the underlying attachment needs for reconnection. This, in turn, generates opportunities for the emotional bonds to form, allowing organizations to achieve ambitious business objectives.[8]

## How to Start the Reconnection

As people begin to share their emotions, fears, and automatic thoughts, the next step in the Process is to identify what they need to feel safe and connected in the moment. EmC is a present-oriented model, as it is not possible to change the past, but rather, it focuses the efforts on repairing the connection to begin the healing process. A cornerstone of the emotional connection is its focus on reassurance and emotional safety as the solid ground for repairs to take place and for the hurt to begin to heal.

Throughout the process, we state what we are hearing, we reframe, and we reassure individuals to create the space for them to share their emotions; to be vulnerable, to be courageous.

As Brené Brown reminds us in her book, *Daring Greatly*,

> Vulnerability isn't good or bad: ... it is the core of all emotions and feelings ... Vulnerability is the cradle of emotions and experiences we crave. Vulnerability is the birthplace of love, belonging, joy, courage, empathy, accountability, and authenticity. If we want greater clarity in our purpose or deeper and more meaningful spiritual lives, vulnerability is the path.[9]

By creating emotional safety, we are thus able to allow vulnerability to emerge and be shared. Focusing on the present, we do not ask about actions or behavioral changes in the future, but rather focus on creating a new emotional experience. For example, we do not ask for promises to be made nor instruct the participants to say, "Promise me you won't do that," or "Don't do that again." Instead, we guide them to engage in an emotional bonding conversation where each person shares their individual emotional experience, while the other participants are able to respond with their empathic presence. This is a critical step that addresses the emotional need and satisfies the longing for connection that was lost in the moment of the disconnect.

### Use Reassuring, Acknowledging Words and Phrases

Research shows that when it comes to reconnection, there are certain basic words and phrases, which provide reassurance and acknowledgment, paving the way to reconnection.[10]

Individuals in conflict need to hear these kinds of statements from each other. In EmC, our goal is to get to the place where one individual is able to tell the other individual their needs and hear statements such as:

1. *I care about you.*
2. *Your feelings are valid.*

3. *What you are saying matters to me.*

4. *You are important to this team.*

5. *I can hear how difficult this was for you in that moment.*

6. *You are valued.*

These and other similar statements address the three most critical needs all humans seek in relationships. We all need to hear and to feel that people we work with care about us, that they value us, and that they will be there for us when we need them.[11]

## How Linda's Team Reconnected—The Bonding Conversations

In the case of Linda and her team, Lola began the reconnection process through the use of these key statements that led to repair and allowed for the bonding conversations to take place. In a series of conversations orchestrated through the EmC process, Lola encouraged direct interaction between Linda and each team member, as each person had been hurt in this situation.

A *bonding conversation* is composed of two steps. In this case, the first step was for each person to share what they needed from Linda to feel safe and connected. The second step was for Linda to actively acknowledge using reassuring statements like those mentioned earlier. Next, Lola, as the facilitator reversed the process by asking Linda what she needed from her team to feel safe and connected. Each team member then had the opportunity to actively respond to her needs. Turning toward the other person and speaking to that person directly is an essential aspect in the enactment, as the words by themselves are not enough, and eye-to-eye contact is necessary to convey emotions and true intentions. If the negative cycle has been influencing a relationship for a long time, it may take a while before it is possible for people to speak directly with each other and to make eye contact. These bonding conversations act to verbally address the needs of all the individuals, but more importantly, they create a new emotional experience, which is felt by everyone at the same time.

In the process, it is important for team members to share some of the positive emotions that they experienced as a result of the bonding conversation. The complete list of positive emotions can be found in Appendix C. There was a palpable change in the dynamics of the room after the bonding conversations. The team members, including Linda, shared feeling excited, humbled, connected, blessed, enthusiastic, confident, safer, optimistic, and relaxed, to name a few reactions. The joy was visible through their smiles, their relaxed laughter, and the overall energy in the room.

### Benefits of the Process

Making positive emotions explicit has the primary effect of expanding the individuals' thinking around their feelings and the equally important effect of creating positive interactions and a general sense of joy and relief. Acknowledging the positive emotions in the room, Lola asked Linda's team for reactions now that they have reconnected:

- *We can create magic together.*
- *We can break the walls down.*
- *We can be there for each other.*
- *We can be stronger together.*
- *We can get our work done faster.*
- *We can make better decisions.*

Linda and her team reached a new emotional experience that allowed them to focus on their needs through facing their fears, which had blocked their attachment and caregiving responses. Not all teams have the experience of arriving at the same place at the end of a session. As such, the process needs to be repeated as many times as necessary for each individual to arrive at a bonding experience. Our work relationships are important to us and play an integral part in our creativity, productivity, and job satisfaction.[12] Negative cycles can be reversed, and a new way of interacting among co-workers and teams can be developed. A new pattern can be integrated into relationships at work. We can build new trust when it is broken. We can change our negative patterns into positive ones.

In a situation where people were extremely distrustful of one another through years of being caught in negative cycles, the EmC process had to proceed at a much slower pace and involved a great deal of effort and time. Since the people were willing to go through the process, it allowed them to repair their relationship and, furthermore, form a more durable connection. Evolution has taught us that we are driven by a strong desire to bond with each other, but we do not always know how to do that when connections break.

## The Sequence of the Positive Cycle

We have seen the pattern of the negative cycle and understand the power of the positive cycle that can emerge. The primary difference, as illustrated in Figure 4.1, between the negative and the positive cycles, is at the moment when the raw spots are triggered, in that moment, the sharing of emotions (softer and primary) and fears and the appropriate caring response, generates a more positive direction to resolving the conflict.

Positive cycles do not in and by themselves eliminate or repair conflicts; people do. The positive cycles allow for people to spend the least amount of time being disconnected. Thus, giving more time in nurturing the bonds people need to risk, reach, and respond in a way that pulls them closer, creating a formidable motivator for change. Through the EmC process, we guide the team to reconnect, enhancing their satisfaction, and widening the opportunities for team members to feel cared about. Experiencing and sharing positive emotions strengthens the positive impact of those emotions and nurtures the bond in relationships.[13]

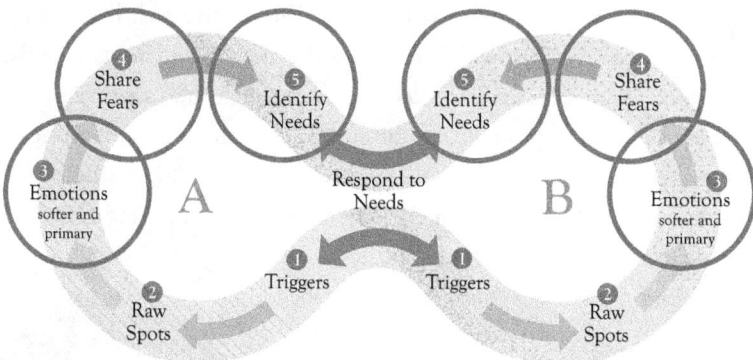

*Figure 5.2 A transformational positive cycle of bonding conversation*

## Questions for Reflection

Here are some questions for you to reflect on:

1. In your personal or work relationships, describe the negative cycle that you have been part of or observed.
2. Identify each person's steps in the negative cycle outlined earlier.
3. What steps would you take to create a positive cycle?

## Summary for Chapter 5

In this chapter, we discussed the emergence of automatic thoughts and subsequent protective behaviors, which accompany negative emotions that are triggered during a conflict. These automatic thoughts and behaviors produce negative cycles that perpetuate the conflict, and over time, if unresolved, create considerable rift and relationship injuries. We identified the three most common negative cycles: attack–withdraw, attack–attack, and withdraw–withdraw. These cycles are often quite difficult to break, and, if allowed to continue, they not only damage team relationships, they create a toxic work culture. The negative cycle becomes a part of the relationship that often permeates individuals' professional and personal lives, limiting their growth and fulfillment.

The EmC process focuses on transitioning from the negative cycle to a positive cycle through methodical reconnection steps that involve the identification of softer and primary emotions, the elucidation of the fears that are present within the individuals in the conflict, and the discussion of the attachment needs that have been lost. The positive cycle begins with a bonding conversation, which addresses the attachment needs directly. The opportunity for individuals to connect through such a conversation initiates the flow of positive emotions, changing the tone and tenor of the connection. Empathy is the lens that illuminates the positive cycle creating stronger bonds within the organization and allowing for more durable relationships.

# CHAPTER 6

# Are You There for Me?: The Magic of A.R.E.

By now, we can see how the EmC process engages team members into structured bonding conversations where each individual can be more vulnerable with emotions. This allows each person to reconnect with the team through a new emotional experience. We have taken a ride through the discovery of emotions and feelings to the point where individuals can recognize the beginning of a negative cycle and, by doing so, turn to each other and express their needs—thus, initiating a positive cycle. Emotions are central to transforming the cycle. The focus on the new interaction heightens the positive impact through creating emotional safety, recognizing value, increasing confidence, and recognizing the importance of connection. These positive emotions increase engagement, support personal and professional growth, and nurture positive and secure bonds within the team.[1]

## Critical Key Concepts

To reach this state of transformation, in addition to the techniques we have covered in the previous chapters, there are key concepts that will assure long-term results by elevating the organization's overall emotional capacity.

### Access Resilience

Resilience gained through the reconnection process can be accessed at all times when we feel disconnected or stressed, uncertain about the times, or vulnerable and fragile. We are capable of working our emotions through envisioning a positive cycle, allowing us to remember the bonding conversations we have had in the past or create new bonding conversations in the future.

### Use a Reassuring Anchor

Our ability to prevent a downward cycle during stressful situations is enhanced by accessing a reassuring anchor in the moment of conflict. This anchor can be a voice or an image that is easily accessible and reassuring. The anchor brings calmness and changes the hormonal balance by increasing the level of oxytocin and reducing the cortisol in our body, thus calming down our heart rate. At this point, the brain is able to relax and regain the emotional balance to address the stress effectively. Research shows that our greatest positive feedback anchors are personal and professional attachment figures such as our partners, family, friends, bosses, co-workers, colleagues, peers, and other key relationships. Turning to these individuals, as appropriate to the situation, provides us with a high and immediate dose of oxytocin.

Our key attachment figures have a profound impact on our nervous system, as we have on theirs. When we have a strong connection with our attachment figures, we are able to regain our balance rapidly and effectively. As an example, from one of the sessions with Linda's team, John stated,

> I'm happy that we can get closer as a team. When I have a stressful situation at work, I can share it with my wife. But, that's never the same as sharing it with my peers who are sitting at this table and can understand what I go through every day. This sharing gets us closer together and gives us a chance to be there for each other. I love that.

### Face the Dragon Together

What we are beginning to understand is how much we need each other to regain our emotional balance, especially with those whom we work with. When we are able to do that consistently with empathy, we are no longer facing the dragon alone; we are at that point, a team committed to building and preserving strong bonds. By creating a secure attachment, we become more confident and collaborative, making it much easier to make good decisions and explore new ideas. We become engaged and optimistic in dealing with various challenges, and we gain emotional responsiveness, the basis of supporting and being supported.[2]

### Are You There For Me?

In the attachment theory terms, the main question our brain focuses on when creating, maintaining, and nurturing a secure bond is: "Are you there for me?" Knowing that the other person (our attachment figure) is there for us in moments of vulnerability is fundamentally what we seek to be emotionally safe, connected, and respond to stressful situations and conflicts. In a study conducted by Susan Johnson, participants received a small electric shock to their ankles while they were holding their partner's hand. The images from the functional Magnetic Resonance Imaging (fMRI) indicated full brain activity as a result of the shock. Some of the participants were enrolled in bonding conversations with their partners, similar to the EmC process, after which the same electric shock experiment was repeated. The results were astonishing. The couples who had been through the bonding conversations—in contrast to those who had not—showed little to no effect on their fMRI as a result of the shock. This study revealed that our perception of threat and our sense of confidence in dealing with that threat is directly proportional to the strength of our emotional bonds.[3]

We see this type of attachment naturally occurring between mothers and children, romantic partners, family members, and strong teams. Bonding conversations such as those in the EmC process attempts to emulate similar attachments. The central code of attachment requires that we have a *felt* sense of security with people we depend on; it cannot be just an idea in our head. As Bowlby pointed out, for us to thrive, we need a safe haven to go to when we are stressed and a secure base to go out from to explore and take risks.[4]

## The Leader's Role

Within Linda's team, Linda is the key attachment figure. This is the case in all teams. The boss is the individual with whom the team members wish to have the strongest possible bond. Through this approach, Linda gained the ability to respond positively to stress, thus creating a safe place for her team members to engage. They were then able to share and express their emotions, fears, and needs with her and with each other. This experience of safety created a felt sense of care, support, and validation, allowing them to be connected. Sharing their vulnerabilities provided the pathway for them to respond to the key bonding questions, "Are you there for me? Do I matter to you?" The responses were a resounding "Yes!"

The EmC process helps to deepen the attachment relationship within the team and promote a culture of care and support. Teams that provide emotional support to each other while sharing their hurts and fears are more likely to develop true alignment between their intentions and emotional cues. Leaders play a critical role in fostering an environment that allows for emotional support and bonding conversations.[5] For example, Linda's leadership intentions were to create safety for her team members; however, her inability to temper her own emotions created undue drama, and her decisions signaled to her team that they did not matter and that they were not important. Her response evoked fear and shame, creating a relationship injury.

The core goal is to lead people in bonding conversations where they can turn to each other and repair their disconnect. Fundamentally, people in secure relationships respond to the question, "Are you there for me?" intuitively in the affirmative when they are in a situational stress point. The EmC is laser-focused on creating relationship repairs and enabling individuals to create strong and durable bonds. As future conflicts are often unavoidable, individuals with secure bonds will be able to ride out the storm with minimal damage to their relationship. This is the principal difference between conflict resolution and the EmC process. Whereas conflict resolution focuses on the immediate conflict, this approach is aimed at restoring emotional connection and thus securing a long-term attachment.

## Promoting Healthy Team Dynamics

In healthy team dynamics, when members have secure bonds with each other, they have each other's backs, and they are *there* for each other. There is an exceptional kind of presence that happens that serves as a powerful safety cue for their brains, powerful enough to turn off stress and fear. When team dynamics are distressed or dysfunctional, individuals are considerably more anxious and disengaged, exhibiting all forms of negative behaviors such as demanding, yelling, ignoring, stonewalling, or being aggressive. Teams can get stuck in repetitive patterns of negative interactions.

### Watch for Warning Signs

Fortunately, there are telltale warning signs that your team may have become so distressed that it is headed down the wrong path. There are two tipping points that determine whether a team is moving toward alienation or into a more secure connection. The first tipping point is to notice when team members are no longer sharing opinions, concerns, and new ideas with each other, thus rendering them less effective in their roles in the organization. The second tipping point is when team members begin to complain, blame, criticize, judge, isolate, disengage, and withdraw, which prevents them from being productive and creative. How leaders respond to these telltale signs determines whether teams and individuals can break the negative patterns and repair their relationships or feed the negative cycle that creates a toxic workplace culture.

## Description of the A.R.E. Tool

A.R.E. is a powerful tool to initiate a positive cycle by providing the necessary ingredients to respond affirmatively and consistently to the question, "Are you there for me?"[6] It is a way of behaving that involves our verbal and nonverbal expressions and our ability to connect emotionally in times of stress. To understand this further, let us break down the components of A.R.E.:

- *Accessible.* It is the ability to be available, open, and attentive to our emotions and those of others when we may also be in the storm of the conflict.
- *Responsive.* It is being emotionally responsive, empathic, and understanding; responding in a manner that acknowledges the emotions of others even when we are stressed ourselves.

- *Engaged.* It is being emotionally engaged with others, not withdrawing or shutting down, not defending or attacking, staying in the conversation.

A.R.E. is most critical for individuals in management and supervisory positions, as the organizational hierarchy dictates a strong longing for attachment between employees and their immediate supervisors. With each of these components, team members learn how to remain accessible, responsive, and engaged so that they can create bonding conversations. Sometimes, it may take a few passes for people to really tune into their emotions and be truly responsive. Our brains are extremely sensitive to visual and auditory cues. Thus, our responses need to go beyond words by making eye contact, facial expressions, and a tone of voice, which convey reassurance and are in alignment with the words we speak. When this does not occur in concert, the other person remains guarded in their actions, and the connection is not repaired. If you think about Ed Tronic's *Still Face Experiment* described in Chapter 3, the moment when the mother began responding to the baby again, she became accessible, responsive, and engaged. Her eyes and her face were open as she looked directly at the baby and was smiling. Nonverbal cues with a calm voice are extremely important in bonding conversations because they calm the brain down.

In the adult world, being A.R.E. does not mean faking a smile and talking baby talk to your colleagues. Instead, it means maintaining good eye contact, keeping your face open, and maintaining a calm voice. This is much harder to do than it sounds; it requires a great deal of practice. It involves the ability to tune in to the emotions behind the words and respond with phrases of understanding, similar to the six responses that were covered in Chapter 4.

When the person we care about is expressing hurt in an overly aggressive manner, it creates a sense of alarm in our brain, and if that person turns and walks away, it triggers feelings of rejection and abandonment. In such moments, we are quite challenged in maintaining our composure. As we become more articulate in identifying our emotions and the emotions of others, we become more skillful in recognizing that behind the anger is pain, behind the turning away is shame, and behind it all is the fear of disconnection. EmC expands our emotional terrain so that we can listen more actively to the emotions of others and share our emotions honestly and openly, staying accessible, responsive, and engaged, thus staying emotionally balanced. Matt Lieberman, the neuroscientist, states that naming emotions accurately starts to change how one responds to others. It calms us down because we are arranging and clarifying our emotional experience, thus allowing us to own our emotions during conflicts and ultimately gain control over our automatic actions.[7] The more we can pinpoint and formulate our emotional experience into clear specific words, the more we can cope. It is then less likely we will become anxious or depressed.[8]

### Use the List of Raw Spots

The List of Raw Spots in Appendix A is a powerful tool in the reconnection process. By giving us the language of emotions, it allows for the ownership process to start, which is critical to entering the positive cycle. Once we can accurately identify our emotions, share each other's raw spots, and be there for each other, we shift to a much better position of solving challenges together. We can think more effectively, communicate more clearly, and break down the walls that arose during the conflict. Becoming accessible, responsive, and engaged is a big part of the second stage, restructuring. It allows individuals start to form and maintain their positive cycles of interaction.

## The Reframing Technique

In taking Linda's team through the process, Lola, as the facilitator, used the attachment framework and the technique of reframing, where she restated what the person had said in attachment terms. The reframing is, in essence, the way to accessibility, responsiveness, and engagement that generate positive cycles during times of stress.

Example:

Linda:  *Ann knew how important that conference call was for me.*

Facilitator:  *Linda, what I am hearing you say is, "Ann, your presence was really important to me. When you didn't show up for the conference call, I worried and panicked. I started to*

| | |
|---|---|
| | *think that what I was asking for was not important to you. I then made a decision for weekly meetings without considering you, and that hurt you. It gave you the message that I didn't care and that you are not important." Linda, I think what you are saying is that Ann is very important to you. Is that correct?* |
| Linda: | *That is absolutely correct.* |
| Facilitator: | *Can you turn and share this with Ann?* |

Turning to Ann, Linda shared the experience directly with Ann while emotionally engaging with her, creating a bonding moment.

Through the reframing, as in the preceding example, Linda demonstrated accessibility, responsiveness, and engagement. Similarly, Ann stated her thoughts and reframing them in attachment terms; they began the reconnection process.

This is, in essence, a shift from the head (content) to the heart (attachment).

As each team member went through the process, the energy in the room changed dramatically from one of stress to one of feeling relaxed and joyful.

All teams are capable of engaging in a way that leads to understanding, engagement, and connection. The longing for connection is in our genes. Each time we can express our feelings and recognize that the disconnect happens naturally because of our emotions, it becomes easier for us to re-engage. We can then step out of the negative cycle and stay connected in an effective way. This allows pursuers to soften their pursuing side and lets withdrawers re-engage and withdraw less. From there, real collaboration takes place, making it possible for all team members to thrive.

## The Science of Emotions

We have been through the emotion and responses in a team, and we have been reflecting on our emotions. We have observed through Linda's team how quickly emotions come and how they influence decisions.

Let us take a deeper dive into the science behind it all.

Dr. Joseph LeDoux at the Center for Neural Science at New York University, in his book, *The Emotional Brain*, provides an examination of how systems in the brain work in response to emotions.[9] LeDoux explains that if we look at the brain structure, we see that the prefrontal cortex, which is responsible for thinking, planning, and the decision-making process, has no direct connection with the emotional region of the brain, the amygdala. However, the amygdala has numerous connections to all brain functions, including the prefrontal cortex. This means that it is easier for our emotions to control our thoughts than it is for our thoughts to control our emotions. Our primary emotions essentially allow the amygdala to hijack the rest of the brain.

When the emotions take over, it becomes difficult for us to communicate, to be open to ideas and collaborate, to stay engaged, and to really understand what the other person is saying or needing.[10] And, it is not just our cognition that slows down; our social skills also diminish. It becomes difficult for us to empathize, to tune into other people's emotions, and to really understand their concerns and pain. When that happens to us, it is a sign that we have lost our emotional balance.

Now that we have discussed the EmC tools (and you have practiced along the way), you can see how it might be able to calm people down in the workplace. If one of our colleagues gets angry, we can immediately call upon our slow-motion camera to observe what is really going on. We know that the colleague's amygdala is essentially hijacking the brain, causing the prefrontal cortex to go off-line, so the person is not able to think clearly.

Emotionally connected leaders understand the science behind disconnections and the importance of attachment. They connect to the real human needs behind the anger and help people regain their emotional balance by remaining accessible, responsive, and engaged, even in the middle of a conflict. They know how to help other people identify their emotions so that they can become creative and productive again.

This is what EmC is all about—through our words, the tone of voice, eye contact, body language, and our ability to talk about underlying emotions, we can help people slow down and regain their emotional balance.

## Questions for Reflection

With the perspective that we can use A.R.E. in all types of situations, think about these questions:

1. Think about a recent conflict. If you could do the conversation over again and use the A.R.E. framework, what would it sound like?
2. Write out your "A.R.E. dialogue" and share it with a partner.

## Summary of Chapter 6

In this chapter, we took a closer look at the central question of "Are you there for me?" as critical to the overall reconnection process.

Deep inside, we are longing for the confirmation that we are supported and valued. We want to feel the safety that is necessary for us to connect with each other during times of vulnerability; we want to fight the dragon together.

In the EmC process, we use the A.R.E. tool, which stands for accessible, responsive, and engaged, exploring the heart of the positive cycle to help people grow and blossom.

We have considered a scientific perspective of how our emotions are in control, as the amygdala influences us in our thoughts and actions. We can learn to calm our brain to respond in a manner that can keep our connections intact and allow us to strengthen our relationships.

Leadership is a constant struggle to maintain a positive perspective in times of uncertainty. As leaders, we are often at a loss as to the correct action when there is much volatility in the environment. Being accessible, responsive, and engaged with our colleagues and employees provides us with a rich set of connections to see our collective way through the many challenges.

# CHAPTER 7

# How to Respond to Emotions

"I had it with my boss! I am tired of being shut down and getting his rolling eyes rejecting every idea I come up with. It makes me feel like I don't know what I am doing. I decided to go and talk to him, to tell him his actions and words are hurtful. What shocked me was his response. He came across as abrupt, dismissive, and accusatory. The sad part is I knew that in his heart, he felt bad. He just didn't know what to say to me and how to respond. So, he just said what was natural to him as a defense mechanism."

A client told Lola this when they met for their initial conversation. It was not the first time she had seen clients hurt by making themselves vulnerable and having responses that appear hurtful and clearly unhelpful. Being conscious of our emotional responses allows us to take ownership of how we respond. To do so, it is essential to learn the slow-motion camera technique for ourselves and then with others as well.

Responding to emotions during conflicts—or even during post-conflict periods—is quite difficult because most of us are trained to respond in a sympathetic manner, using statements such as, "Oh, I am sorry you feel that way," or "I didn't mean to hurt your feelings," or "Tell me why you are feeling this way?" Unfortunately, those responses are not empathetic because they do not acknowledge the feelings being expressed. A more productive response would be to focus just on those feelings and emotions, slowly exploring with the individual the state they are in. By retraining ourselves to slow everything down, we can feel what is being expressed and thus respond empathetically.

To explore this point and illustrate how this can work in real life, we want to share an experience Lola had with one of her teams some time ago.

## Responding to Emotions: A Real-Life Example

In a meeting with the whole team, as the conversation began to heat up, Lola felt she was being dismissed and not heard. Her immediate response was to shut down to the point where she could not comprehend what others were saying. She suddenly felt as if she was on the edge of a cliff while everyone else was sitting in comfortable chairs on the other side. Instead of withdrawing from the group, Lola reached out to the team, and shared what she was feeling at that moment. Fortunately, one of her colleagues, who was skilled in EmC, asked, "*What do you need right now to feel safe and connected?*"

"I need to know that my feelings are valid," Lola responded.

Without any hesitation, he validated her feelings, and in that very instant, she felt a shift. She was not on the edge of a cliff anymore. They were able to re-engage and had a productive and creative meeting. It is important to note that in all moments of conflict or significant reactions to something that has been said, such as the two cases described, there are a complex set of emotions in play, which trigger a number of reactions, all centered on our fears. It takes time to learn and perfect the slow-motion camera technique and to be prepared to absorb the emotional tsunami.

Our goal is to be able to ask and answer questions (such as the one noted earlier), which are simple in nature but rich in their expression of empathy and elicitation of responses that are emotionally authentic. Knowing our own emotions and sharing them openly and honestly without making judgments or accusations takes a great deal of practice. Doing so allows us to exercise empathy in all situations, whether as the pursuer or as a withdrawer. The EmC process is an experiential approach that takes time and commitment to master.

## The Five Techniques

The road to gaining deep emotional connection within teams is built using statements that convey value, importance, acceptance, validation, and connection. In the EmC process, we accomplish this using a method we call The Five Techniques. These techniques allow us to respond and lead participants through the experiential process, where they are able to heighten their connection with each other. As with any technique, at first, The Five Techniques may seem to be prescriptive and ingenuine. But, they are simply like dance instructions for a new type of dance, one you have not done before. As you practice the new dance steps to the new music, you learn to more organically use these techniques and tune in to the other people on the dance floor. The end results are fluid and natural movements and interactions.

These five techniques are:

1. Emotional responsiveness
2. Validation
3. Empathic reflection
4. Normalizing
5. Reframing

Let us talk about each technique in detail.

### Emotional Responsiveness

Emotional responsiveness is not content-based but instead focuses on the person's emotions and the difficulty he or she is experiencing at that moment. Emotional responsiveness with team members can play a significant role in positively responding to stressful situations and helping those who get caught in a negative cycle of conflict. A study of 300 undergraduate students found those who perceived emotional responsiveness from their significant others were less likely to experience disengagement, dysfunction, and distress.[1] In his attachment theory, Bowlby points out that when we experience stress or threat, we seek empathy as a way of regulating our negative emotions such as fear or sadness.[2]

In the EmC process, we focus on connecting to people's emotions rather than trying to fix their problems. Through using the emotional responsiveness technique, we create an environment of psychological safety. This helps everyone's brain to relax, which allows for open and transparent dialogue. In the case of Linda, if we would have tried to explain to her that she over-reacted, most likely, Linda would have felt judged and dismissed. Instead, using the technique of emotional responsiveness (e.g., by acknowledging her feelings), we created a secure base for her to mitigate her stress and increase her ability to cope with her fear of feeling unimportant. Empathy is an essential component of emotional responsiveness. Empathy is the ability to understand, share, and tolerate the feelings of another person as he or she experiences emotional pain. It is important to know the difference between empathy and sympathy. Sympathy often sounds like this: "Linda, it's terrible that this happened to you. Well, at least some of your team members showed up."

We all have experienced it: the moment when we share something painful and others just minimize or dismiss it. In their attempt to make us feel better, they try to explain the situation or suggest we should look at the bright side and be grateful. While this a noble attempt at help, unfortunately, most often, this makes us feel even worse than before because our emotional underpinning has not been acknowledged. Instead of minimizing the stress reaction, we use empathy where we can say, "I can see how difficult that was for you. I can hear that this was really important to you." Through emotional responsiveness, we support people in order to hear and understand the difficult experience they feel so that they can be heard and understood.

### Validation

Validation is all about affirmation and helping people legitimize their emotional experience. With a simple phrase, such as "your feelings are valid," we are confirming the emotion, not necessarily the content, reaction, or any other component. Doing so allows the individual to not have to defend their emotions, but instead, feel the safety of sharing and gaining acceptance. Another good validation phrase is: "I understand why you would respond this way." This is most effective when people have shared their automatic thoughts and protective behaviors. Acknowledging the response, not necessarily the content of the response, allows us to empathize with the fear and panic that proceeded a particular action or decision (as with Linda's case). Validation phrases regulate people's emotions by reassuring them that their feelings are important and real; that their reactions are understandable. In moments when someone feels vulnerable, our proper response says to the other person, "You are safe with me. I've got you." If we focus on explaining with logic, reasons, and arguments, we invalidate their experience and create more disconnection at a deeper level: wrong channel, wrong time. Talking about logic or explanation during the time when people are emotionally stressed most often only adds to their stress.

Managers are attachment figures in teams and have the power to manage the emotional alarms among the members of their teams. Validation allows the managers not to dismiss the threat being perceived by their employees but rather diminish the danger that could come from it. It is like being a guide leading someone on a hike through the jungle. When we encounter a rushing river, the person feels afraid. But because we have been here before, we can point out a path through the river and lead them across, one stone at a time. Validation phrases are like those stepping stones. Each time we validate people's feelings, it helps diminish their stress, and their confidence begins to grow. As they identify and articulate their feelings, they feel less overwhelmed, and they start to let their self-protective guard down. When we use validation, we pay attention to the facial expressions, body language, and tone of voice by using the slow-motion camera. We slowly repeat things because we know that when people are stressed, their brains do not process the information as quickly as when they are calm and relaxed.

### Empathic reflection

Reflection is a common technique to verify what is being said. In the EmC process, we use empathic reflection with statements such as, "Let me see if I understand this correctly," or "What I'm hearing you say is ..." These statements allow us to slow down the emotions. At the same time, we can gauge the accuracy of what we have heard, creating the feeling of being heard. Empathic reflection also can give us the opportunity to repeat important points that clarify the message. We absorb the person's experience by tracking and reflecting the poignant emotions and redirecting the focus from content to the emotional experience. Empathic reflection allows people to gain distance from their emotions. We want people to clarify their emotions so that they can be in touch with them and not be overwhelmed by them.

## Normalizing

Normalizing is a crucial step in the EmC process. We use statements such as, "It is normal to feel this way," or "We all have felt the way you are feeling now." Sharing emotions is vulnerable and uncomfortable because it is generally unconventional to discuss emotions in the workplace. Think of a time when you took the risk of sharing hurt feelings. What was that experience like for you? Did you feel anxious or worried? How did people respond to you? Was it a positive or a negative experience? Did you feel better or worse afterward?

When we normalize people's feelings and experiences, we help them to feel safe and supported. We assure them that feeling as they do is normal and not weak or pathetic as they may think. The feelings are evoked when the individual loses the connection to the people they depended on. The normalizing technique serves as a great regulator. It makes people feel supported, accepted, and normal when they share emotions. It acknowledges that emotions are present for all individuals, as feelings are an essential presence in all humans. When we normalize during times of stress, we send the message that sharing vulnerability is healthy and universal, leading to greater safety and more effective connections.

## Reframing

Reframing is, in essence, a reorientation process guiding the individuals in conflict toward a framework of caring or defeating a common enemy such as the negative cycle. Principally, the most common attachment anchor is that of caring for each other and for the organization. We reframe the conversations between individuals to point out the critical common point between them. In the beginning, they may feel that they care about different things, but ultimately, the fact that they are in conflict indicates that they share a strong desire to connect with each other. Repeated reframing, along with the other techniques discussed earlier, allows for arrival at a common critical juncture necessary for reconnection.

As Linda became more facile with the EmC process and the reframing technique, she was able to change the dynamics of her team interactions during times of disconnect. As an example, she recalled a time when on a conference call, the conversation seemed to be headed in the wrong direction and was becoming more confrontational. Linda sensed the disconnect and reframed the situation by saying,

> Could we pause for a second? I can sense the passion that you all have about this topic. I know how much you all care about this project. And how much you care about each other. I just wanted to say that.

After the conversation resumed, the tone was different, people started to listen to each other, and they were able to come to a collaborative decision that everyone agreed with.

In the preceding example, Linda used the technique of reframing around the common attachment point of caring for the organization and for each other. At times, especially in cases where the conflict is deep and long term where individuals are emotionally incapable of focusing on positive attributes, such as caring, we use the common attachment point of defeating the negative cycle as the focus. We make statements such as, "It sounds like you are caught in a terrible negative cycle," or "The negative cycle is taking over your relationship." The goal becomes helping the two individuals to pivot toward understanding the negative cycle between them and eliminating the cycle through their collective effort. We reorient the individuals away from blaming each other to align them both against the negative cycle so that they can both work toward the same goal. They become part of a team that is now pursuing one unifying objective.

### Affirmation Statements

Affirmation statements help people feel stronger as they go through the process. These statements acknowledge the courage and strength in sharing feelings and thoughts. It is not easy to share vulnerability in the open and especially with a person with whom one has a disconnect. With the affirmation statements, we acknowledge being moved by their effort to fight for their relationship and see how much they care. These statements may sound like this: "I can see how much this matters to you," and "I feel honored that you would share this with me." Some other affirmation statements include: "I am amazed by your courage and strength to be able to work through the struggle" and "I saw how tuned in you were, even while you were saying, 'I'm not sure how to do this.'"

Affirmation statements need to be repeatedly spoken as each step of the process creates different vulnerabilities and fears. They are a tool to help support people by creating a safe and understanding environment.

## We Can Rewrite Our Conflict Narrative

The turning point in long-standing conflicts is when we stop focusing on the rational arguments in order to seek solutions, and instead, focus on recognizing the emotional underpinnings of the conflict and the negative cycles that are operating underneath. The reframing of the narrative centers around gaining a deeper understanding of the cycle of blaming and experiencing repeated hurts from being rejected and abandoned. Instead, we help team members focus on the desire for connection.

The EmC process is, at its core, a reframing tool—giving teams, individuals, and leaders the necessary framework for genuine and authentic conversations around feelings and emotions, which are inflamed during moments of stress. It addresses the underpinnings of conflict, thus giving people the chance to rewrite negative patterns that would otherwise persist into the future. Struggling teams often share certain desperation and a firm belief that their conflict will never be resolved. We often hear, "We've tried it all; we can't see a way out." From experience, what we have observed is that most efforts are focused on finding a solution without serious involvement of emotions, which often leads to discouragement and exhaustion. A solution-focused orientation is a wrong perspective. It takes significant amounts of energy without producing a result because, underneath, it is primarily a process of connection between individuals that is broken and must be repaired.

# Questions for Reflection

The following questions may help you to think through the concepts in this chapter.

1. Think of a situation where you and someone else had a disconnect. How would it feel if you and the other person would engage in an emotionally responsive conversation with each other?
2. How would your conversation change if you were to validate each other's feelings?
3. What would empathic reflection sound like?
4. How would it feel to normalize each other's emotions?
5. What do you think would happen to your relationship if there was a reframing of the feelings involved? Would you anchor around the common points of care, or would you focus on reorienting the blame on the negative cycle?

# Summary of Chapter 7

The EmC process makes available the language needed to have a detailed discussion of feelings and emotions that we experience during moments of conflict. It emphasizes the process of becoming conscious of our emotional responses and taking ownership of how we respond. We learned how to properly address emotions and give space when they are shared by being present and responsive during moments of vulnerability. We introduced five techniques that can be used to respond to emotional reactions. These help us move away from content and focus on the underlying emotions, thereby generating the safety and understanding necessary for the bonding conversations to take place. We demonstrated how important affirmation statements are in rebuilding the attachment and making the bond stronger, thus creating a feeling of safety and understanding.

Through using these techniques, we can interrupt the negative cycle and prevent it from spinning out of control, thus allowing us to rewrite the narrative, which accompanies most conflicts.

# CHAPTER 8

# Forming a Holistic Strategy Through EmC

Years ago, on a trip to Costa Rica, walking through the rain forest, Lola recalled an important lesson she learned. The guide suddenly stopped her asking her not to move.

"Look four inches from your right foot."

Lola looked, but there was nothing there. There were just a whole bunch of leaves. It is a rain forest!

"I can't see anything other than leaves," Lola said.

"Look! The thing you think is a stick is a long tail. The thing you think is a stone is an eye. That is a nightjar."

The nightjar is a bird that nests on the floor of the forest. It was four inches away from Lola's foot, and she could not see it until her guide pointed it out.

## Seeing the Nightjars in Human Relationships

This is similar to what we experience when sitting in long meetings. We observe and, at times, participate in what appears to be long cycles of explanations, understandings and misunderstandings, miscommunications, accusations, and eventual disengagements. We wonder greatly—what will solve these problems? Should we change or improve the contents, the mannerisms, the hierarchy, the expertise, or the meeting structure? However, we rarely ask about the emotions underneath. The nightjars in human relationships that we often fail to see—especially at the workplace—are the emotions that are present in each and every interaction. Most often, we attempt to *fix* the problem by clarifying using many words, frustrating each other by persuasion, explanation, and more information. These attempts drive people apart as pursuers step up and attack, and the withdrawers pull back. Both pursuers and withdrawers do what they do with the best of intentions to keep the connection, not realizing that their actions send the wrong signals to the other person.

In our daily relationships, we get triggered into actions and, because emotions occur quickly, the disconnect occurs before we even realize it. From there, the chain reaction in our brain generates automatic thoughts that quickly translate to protective behaviors that diminish creativity, slow down our cognition, and, ultimately, lead to less productivity. Companies and organizations are not immune to the winds of change, whether they come in the form of market conditions, global trends, or management transitions. In the wake of all these, the stress on individuals, their teams, and their hierarchical relationships are high and volatile. Triggers are seemingly around every corner, and automatic thoughts permeate the daily work environment.

The EmC, as a strategy, is capable of going beyond simple conflict management to engage people during times of high stress and help them become aware of their emotions and the opportunity they all have to create positive cycles that embrace the change and allow them to thrive. Secure bonds impact not just relationships but the individuals themselves. In a Harvard Study over the course of 80 years, researchers found a strong correlation between connection and health.[1] People who are connected are much happier, feel better about themselves, talk in a more defined and positive way, feel stronger, are better able to deal with stress, and have greater resilience in life than those who are disconnected.

## When Other Approaches Do Not Work

In the face of dysfunction, discord, ineffective meetings, poor performance, and so on, we have all worked to bring solutions such as communication skills, negotiation skills, management improvement plans, retreats, and so on. Yet, we are incapable of stopping the conflicts, and moreover, we are often struggling to understand why the conflicts are occurring in the first place. We both eventually learned that the fighting was not due to the lack of certain skills or missing reflection time. The problem was that something much more important was at stake: survival, attachment, and emotional safety.

As we have discussed thus far, our desire for attachment and emotional connection is akin to dancing with our colleagues. While it is always our intention to dance together, disagreements have the ability to change the dynamics where each individual's emotions can create different music and different dances; one does the polka and the other the tango. In large groups with powerful players, there can be as many different dances as there are people in the room. We even witness individuals who literally take themselves off the dance floor by fully disengaging. It is indeed the act of withdrawal that causes dysfunction—and inversely, the connection is what enables cohesion. Emotional connection is far greater than content; it is visceral and deep.

## EmC and Leadership

Leadership in organizations emanates out of courage to meet the challenges while caring for people and giving them a chance to thrive in their quest to meet business and social objectives. The courage is fortified through healthy attachment relationships that leaders have throughout their companies. Courage becomes infectious, as connections are strengthened within teams and individuals. In the EmC process, much of the attention is given to negative emotions or negative cycles; however, the EmC process is also a great tool for generating bonding conversations to repair and strengthen the connections. Natural leaders do this by instinct, and others can use the EmC as a strategy to gain a new capacity for healthy connections and achieve sustainable relationship success.

Leadership is the art of understanding and caring for those the leader has the privilege of leading. Like all people, leaders struggle with understanding their own emotions, verbalizing their vulnerability, and maintaining emotional balance—especially during times of great uncertainly and volatility. The struggle itself is healthy, as it forces self-reflection, self-acceptance, and self-discovery; the finding of one's courage is often preceded by these moments of the inward journey. The result of understanding oneself allows leaders to be far more effective and compassionate in leading their organizations. The EmC as a strategy partners with leaders to harness the power of emotions to change the dynamics when people are caught in turbulence.

As we have learned in previous chapters through the A.R.E. conversations, what people seek more than anything else during times of disconnection or stress is the notion that their leaders are accessible, responsive to their needs, and are positively engaged in guiding them through the uncertainty. When people are valued and cared for, they are capable of achieving extraordinary results even at the worst of times. Moreover, they will do so with cohesion and camaraderie that will strengthen over time. Their resilience and innovation are supercharged, and that is good for everyone.

## The Experiential Nature of the EmC Process

Albert Einstein said, "All knowledge is experience, everything else is just information." We are inundated with a plethora of training programs centered around great information and knowledge; however, very few provide us the experiences through the learning process that cements the changes necessary for us to thrive.

These programs are mostly didactic in nature based on information exchange, with the expectation that once the employee knows the content, they will change their behavior. It is assumed that knowing is the same as doing; however, it is understanding emotions that is the ultimate driver of behavior, culminating behavior change. In essence, a traditional training program and their engagemenet sets up a negative cycle, where an employee and their engagement is considered to be the problem results in little or no progress. That individual is then eventually terminated, and the problem is silenced until the next time it occurs with another individual, and the cycle repeats itself. The organizational costs and the financial burden of continuous negative cycles are staggering.

In contrast to traditional training programs, the EmC process is, by nature, experiential. Through its methodical and compassionate approach, it draws participants into a dialogue that allows them to recognize their emotions and those of the others—and actively work toward connection and repair.[2] The re-engagement of individuals, in realtime and in the present, is essential to the long-term behavioral change necessary for improved performance on the job. Based on the notion of creating a new emotional experience, the EmC process slowly and reassuringly helps individuals travel the path of connection for themselves and others involved. During moments of great stress, the brain is not cognitively oriented but rather instinctually responding to situations for survival.

With EmC, individuals move from slowing the automatic negative responses and instead are able to create emotionally healthy interactions that help them repair the relationship. We begin the process by orienting the situation to the present moment. This starts the moment we focus on emotions as opposed to other methodologies that concentrate on the content of the situation or disconnect. By identifying emotions at that instant, we automatically place everything in the present. By contrast, discussions of *content* emphasize the past and give permission for blame, defense, and other negative strategies.

In the EmC process, the emotional reality begins to shift with questions such as, "What happened here?" or "What emotions did you feel at that moment?" and "What message did it give you?" Identifying and thereby owning one's emotions is the first step on this new journey. The intensity of the emotions and the holistic nature of the conflict is best explored through asking individuals to create the image that describes them in that moment of stress. It is not the quality of the image that matters, but rather, what people include in the image, how they position themselves and others, and what story they attribute to the image.

The experience is further solidified automatic thoughts and behaviors that are generated as a result of the emotions, in both the present and what may have been there during the conflict. Understanding how the amygdala, in essence, has hijacked our responses becomes an essential feature of experiencing our own lack of cognitive control during moments of stress. Linda realized that her decision to hold weekly meetings as a result of her discontent was entirely an emotional response driven from her automatic thoughts and protective behaviors. Clarifying her emotions and owning them opened her eyes to see that she had been a victim of hijacking that led her into a giant negative cycle with her team. This self-realization is most effective when experienced as part of this process. Consequently, when done correctly, individuals experience the presence of the negative cycle. It is the cycle that is now real and identifiable that is responsible for their continuous disconnect; a new enemy is now visible to the team. With the negative cycle now fully understood and the emotions and thoughts clarified, the experience is enriched through the enactment of words and phrases and eye contact, which create the opportunity for bonding conversations to occur.

The process clearly helps drive individuals to face each other when they are ready to reconnect. Through these bonding conversations, individuals are able to clarify their hurt and seek reassurance from the other person. The vulnerability created through this action generates an authentic experience felt by everyone in the room; its power is limitless in how it can repair and, eventually, strengthen the bond. The human experience is not lived in a vacuum. It is the combination of the contextual and emotional envelope that creates the experience or our perceptions of it. These steps create a safe and reassuring environment that allows individuals room for vulnerability. It relies a great deal on reassuring concepts, repetition, and reframing, all done to ensure individuals feel heard and understood (Figure 8.1).

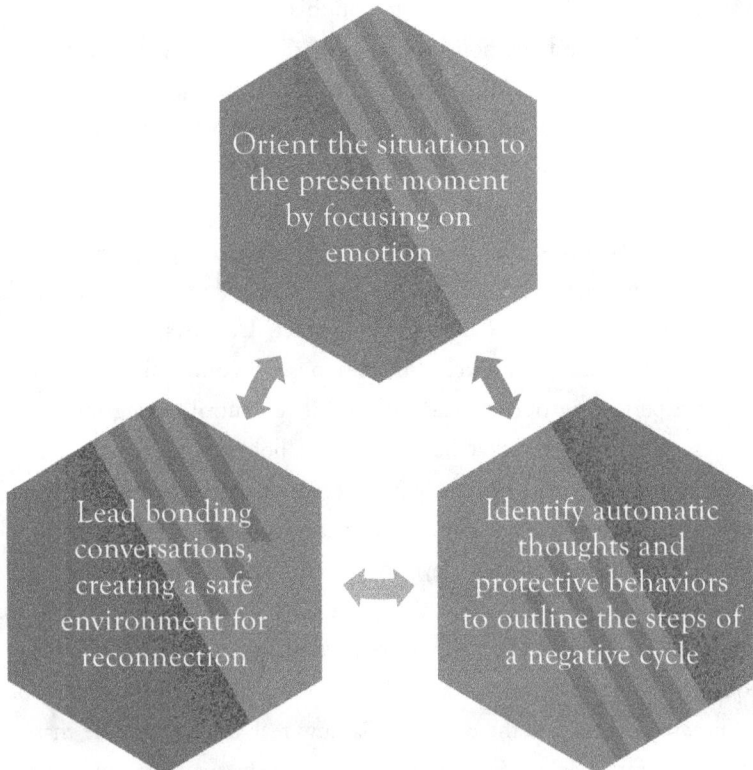

Orient the situation to the present moment by focusing on emotion

Lead bonding conversations, creating a safe environment for reconnection

Identify automatic thoughts and protective behaviors to outline the steps of a negative cycle

Figure 8.1 Reconnection process

## The Importance of Repetition

The EmC process, once fully acquired and regularly practiced, becomes essential during stressful interactions. While we see the immediate changes, the effect of attachment and reconnection takes time; thus, repetition is critical in creating the full experience. Why? Because our brains do not function well when emotions are high. Our capacity to receive clear messages through listening is reduced; thus, repetition allows us to process the information and to properly engage with the other person. When people are sharing their emotions, as facilitators, we slow things down by repeating what we are hearing and what we are observing. Recognition of emotions is significant, as it helps people to regulate their emotions and not feel bombarded by them. Repetition slows down the process giving everyone a chance to digest the emotional experience. Leaders who are able to navigate the stress moment, through repetition and reassurance, make connections and create safety.

Reframing the negative cycle allows leaders to focus the conflict away from blame and defensiveness by continuously repeating phrases such as, "I know how much everyone cares about this project. It sounds to me like a negative cycle has taken over, leaving everyone feeling alone." To move people away from blaming each other to blaming the negative cycle is difficult when people experience pain. It is hard for them to accept the fact that each individual took part in perpetuating the negative cycle. The negative cycle is usually very strong because it has taken over the daily interactions, and as such, it feeds a great deal of hostility and anger, followed by stonewalling or explosion. People have no trust in each other, everyone is labeling everyone else, and there is no openness or emotional balance.

The EmC process creates space for safety through repetition, which slows down the cycle. In turn, repetition has the additional benefit of allowing leaders to maintain their emotional balance during conflicts, so they can be effective in recognizing the negative cycles in play. Doing so prevents leaders from getting caught up in the actual conflict or focusing too greatly on the content. Repetition acts as a regulator during the reconciliation process as the music heard by different people is allowed to harmonize into an experience that can be shared. This, in turn, provides the framework for repairing the connection. The underlying principle of

EmC rests on the attachment connection we all seek. It is the repetition inherent in the process that allows for the articulation of the threats, vulnerability, primal panic, and the helplessness felt at times of stress. By making the implicit feelings explicit through repetition, we initiate the shift to change the perspective and reduce panic and desperation, thus restructuring the negative cycle into a positive. From the moment we start the process to the moment that we end, we use all of the techniques repeatedly to create and sustain the momentum for change.

The EmC as a strategy equips leaders with an entirely different perspective as if each leader is given a powerful microscope able to penetrate the emotional underpinning of the disconnections in their teams. Our softer and primary emotions are invisible to the naked eye and, as such, are often neglected in addressing conflicts and stress. Indeed, just as Lola missed seeing the nightjar in the jungle at work, we usually miss the fact that it is our desire for attachment with people that is essential in our personal or professional lives—and that it is the crux of all of our disengagements and conflicts. The deliberate process, through its myriad of techniques—repetitions, reframing, normalizing, emotional responsiveness, validation, and reflection—provides the set of lenses that allow us to see, understand, and repair what truly matters. The courage needed for leadership and for change is strengthened; the more we are able to form enduring bonds and channel the conflicts through positive cycles, the greater our ability to honor the emotions and the passions of the people we work with.

## Questions for Reflection

In reflecting on this chapter, here are a few questions to think about:

1. Can you recall an instance where you observed your own *nightjar?* Describe the circumstance and the feelings you had upon such a discovery.
2. In your own work as a leader, can you recall various methodologies you have used in addressing conflicts or disconnections? Describe how they impacted your relationships and the organization.

3. Take one of the methodologies and think through your experience as it unfolded. How engaged were you during the process? Focus primarily on your emotional engagement.

## Summary of Chapter 8

In this chapter, we learned through the nightjar story that we are unable to see what we have not been trained to observe and, as a result, miss the beauty that surrounds us. In the case of conflicts, the beauty is the longing for connection, which, having been severed, is expressed through the negative emotions of the participants. The EmC is by design and necessity an experiential process determined to create the safety necessary for individuals to recognize, identify, and share the emotions they are feeling in the present. They are then able to experience the triggers and the raw spots, which generate automatic thoughts and protective behaviors resulting in continuous negative cycles. The EmC strategy is the integration of the EmC process and mindset into the organizational structure and the leadership culture.

Leaders, by virtue of their roles, are called upon during times of stress. Conflicts and disengagements are particularly toxic to the organization's productivity, creativity, and overall health. Using the EmC as a strategy, leaders have the opportunity to turn negative cycles into positive engagements. They do this by maintaining their own emotional balance, while at the same time, creating an environment honoring the passions and emotions of their teams.

In leadership, making deep and meaningful connections is the special ingredient that allows for people to achieve vitality and growth, the critical ingredients for thriving.

# CHAPTER 9

# How to Address Common Challenges

In our path toward emotional connection, there are numerous challenges that can prevent us from making progress. Many of the business books currently used to educate managers about communication, leadership, or human interactions in the workplace ignore the role emotions play in determining actions and reactions. Most often, they concentrate on methodologies based on contextual understanding of issues, communication strategies to improve discourse, and performance enhancement plans to remediate employee deficiencies. By ignoring emotions, we lay the foundation for team dysfunction. Conversely, by acknowledging emotions, we build the framework for high-functioning teams, regardless of context or content.

In fact, many of us have been taught that discussing or acknowledging emotions in the workplace is, at best, inappropriate and, at worst, highly unproductive. Ironically, at the same time, there has been an increase in recognizing concepts such as empathic leadership, which emphasizes connections, bonds, and psychological safety. Despite our best intentions, the big challenge is still all the destructive aspects of organizational disconnects, as seen in hierarchy, deep cycles of negativity, board pressures, animosity, and unenlightened human resources structures.

The EmC strategy has the potential to play a critical role in connecting the empathic leader to their organization by generating the thoughts and actions that are centered on emotional connections. It is only then that the much sought-after creativity and innovation, productivity and quality, and engagement and thriving occur. In the last 20 years, developmental and social psychologists have realized the power of a secure bond with another person—the power of knowing that someone has our back, the feeling we have that we are important to others on our team and that we can turn to them. This secure bond has a considerable impact on our nervous system, brain function, and, subsequently, creativity.[1] The science of neuroplasticity tells us that through these emotional experiences, the brain develops new bonds and pathways to respond differently to threats and stress.[2]

With the EmC strategy people can experience a new way to build points of contact to connect and interact. The ruptured bond that creates aloneness and helplessness is the core element present in a toxic environment. The premise behind EmC is the invitation to look at situations from a different perspective—where *being unstuck* and emotional growth takes place all at once, in tandem. Having said all this, we realize that under even the best circumstances, positive cycles of interaction are interrupted or diverted by several common interpersonal challenges. Let us take a closer look at them now.

## Trust

Trust is most often cited as critical to individual and organizational success. It is the lack of trust within teams, peers, bosses, and direct reports, which, when present, prevents healthy and positive interactions. When we do not trust or feel we are not trusted, our raw spots are triggered more often, and our automatic responses feed our suspicions, resulting in rapid judgments and disconnections. This negative cycle further erodes trust if it continues and is not repaired.

While trust can be content-based, it is fundamentally the connection built and nurtured between individuals. The lack of trust presents itself as an obstacle as the team proceeds through the EmC process. Thus, it is critical to address and remedy the trust necessary for individuals to engage fully in bonding conversations. In situations where there is a clear lack of trust on the part of the participants or in the system, the EmC process takes an extremely slow approach and not necessarily in the sequence that has been described in prior chapters. Individuals need the time and space to gain basic comfort in interacting with each other, such as simply being in the room together or talking about their softer emotions. The slower the speed of the reconnection process, the more likely they will share elements that can then be harvested to facilitate the next steps in the process. Here is an example of how this might go:

*A session has been set up with Sean and Mark, who are clearly not working well together. Sean asked for the session to be postponed on the day of the session, leaving Mark bewildered. While this may be a typical withdrawer and pursuer situation, upon closer inspection, we learn of Sean's deep lack of trust in Mark.*

*In his attempt to keep moving forward, Mark suggests the session should go on since the hour is late, and the facilitator is on the scene.*

*Sean arrived late for the session. At this moment, the facilitator could have gone forward with the EmC process as prescribed. However, that would have been fruitless. Instead, the facilitator used the opportunity to ask Sean, "What is it like when Mark wants to have a session, and you don't?"*

*Reflecting and validating Sean's response is a critical step in paving the road to re-engagement.*

*The facilitator then asks Mark, "What is it like for you when Sean wants to cancel the sessions?"*

*In this volley of questions and answers, we learn that Sean feels overwhelmed by the number of questions and the intensity of Mark's pursuit, whereas Mark feels alone.*

*Sean, hearing Mark's response to feeling alone, and Mark hearing Sean's response of feeling overwhelmed, created a moment where they each experienced the other's vulnerability. In particular, Sean was moved by how much Mark cared about him, a powerful empathic response, where trust became possible once again.*

Through our experience and validated by research, those who have difficulty with emotional engagement and avoid sharing their vulnerabilities are shown to be less effective in building trust with their colleagues.[3] At work, often, these people find comfort in focusing on tasks rather than on building relationships. Teams that learn to be emotionally open and responsive with each other improve not just their feelings of emotional connection but create a higher level of trust in their working relationships (see Table 9.1). Cultural and family structures have a great deal of influence on people's behavior in the workplace, and while some cultures emphasize assertiveness, others emphasize a more compliant approach. These differences are accommodated by allowing individuals to guide their journey at their own pace. The key to building and preserving trust is through the heart by engaging in emotional connection and responsiveness.

*Table 9.1 Emotional connection and enhancing trust*

| Challenge | Remedy |
|---|---|
| Lack of Trust | • Slow down the EmC process<br>• Reflect and validate<br>• Engage in emotional responsiveness |

### Alignment

In teams and among people who work together, there exists a hidden trap, that of alignment. We take great effort in recruiting and hiring people who share our values and expectations. We consider it a plus if the candidate shares our particular approach and agenda for the team and organization. However, what do we know about the values, expectations, and often evolving agendas of the people who we already work with? Moreover, if the working relationship has not been strong or has been in continuous conflict, the chances of misalignment are high. Misalignment or the perception of it can create a significant obstacle as one deploys the EmC process or, for that matter, any attempt at meaningful workplace connections. Similar to trust, recognition and positive reconciliation of alignment issues will allow for long-term effectiveness. We focus solely on the key statements made by the individuals as they describe their particular situation or disconnection.

The facilitator typically would ask, "What happened?"

A typical response would be,

*We've talked about how this should be done, and it just keeps being done wrong. And then on top of it, she gives me an attitude when I tell her that it was not good enough. How can she do that? Doesn't she know any better? I would never talk to my boss like that.*

In this example, we see the intensity of the response, which begins with an exasperated and blaming scenario, which includes passing judgment on the employee. This is typically the indication of misalignment of values and expectations. Blaming and judgment are the primary responses in situations of misalignment. By being tuned to these phrases and their repeated presence in the early parts of the conversation, we can become more aware that there are fundamental issues at play requiring attention and work.

Values are the most fundamental of the misalignment challenges, and so it is critical to clarify them in the process. A skillful facilitator will quickly help individuals, especially in situations of blaming and judging, to focus away from the other person and look inside themselves. That helps individuals recognize the role they play that involves their internal values. It also provides them and the facilitator with three possible perspectives. The primary perspective is that by exploring one's values, individuals realize that during the heat of the negative cycle, their automatic thoughts and behaviors were inconsistent with their value systems. This often happens as emotions take over our cognitive abilities to discern the right way of acting according to our principles. Secondarily, exploration of values, especially during this time of stress, can reveal that the individuals in conflict either share the same values or have differing principles as to relationships and attachment. In the first case of sharing the same values, the process of reconciliation is greatly facilitated, as it becomes a matter of working through the emotions to arrive at the bonding conversations. In the unfortunate case, when there are clearly different value systems in place, individuals can openly see the differences having worked through their emotions and are then able to make better decisions about reconciliation, reconnection, and future relationships. In cases of differing values, the transparency of this process will allow individuals to make decisions as to whether they will remain with the organization or decide to part ways. In either case, the relationship is saved. Here is a real-life example to demonstrate the point:

*A CEO who worked with Lola years ago had great difficulty with his board. While seemingly the challenges were typical, as Lola worked through the emotions (which took numerous sessions), the CEO eventually arrived at a "value" impasse. The CEO decided to leave the company because it had become clear that he and the board had significant differences in their values system. Learning this through a Process aimed at connection and the human need for attachment allowed the CEO to part ways while at the same time develop a new relationship with board members.*

Values, expectations, and agendas can clearly differ from one person to another, making team relationships complex. The process of realignment as described in Table 9.2, involves taking steps to identify and recognize values, expectations, and agendas at an emotional level—where their influence is most clearly seen and understood—allows individuals to re-engage with each other authentically.

**Table 9.2 Emotional connection and improving alignment**

| Challenge | Remedy |
|-----------|--------|
| Alignment | • Move away from blaming<br>• Focus inside of yourself<br>• Explore your values<br>• Evaluate automatic thoughts and protective behaviors to align with your values |

## Awareness

Have you had an experience when what you said to someone came across to them as negative and caused harm when you did not mean it that way? Most of us do not intend to harm others with our responses, certainly not deliberately, not even when the impulse is an attack from a protective behavior. However, the impact of our actions on another person can be quite significant and different from what was intended. Becoming aware of how sensitive we are when we depend on someone whom we work with helps us to stay aware of how facial expressions can be interpreted by someone else as painful or dangerous or hurting, or how our tone of voice can be a trigger, taking attention away from the content of the conversation. If the reaction one receives is disproportionate and distorted in relation to the original statement, question, or action, one needs to stop and evaluate what is behind the reaction. By asking a simple question such as, "What just happened here?" we stand to learn important information about the context in which the other person acts. We also gain an understanding of underlying issues that may relate to the current disconnection or to a previous workplace, life, or relationship trauma.

Unresolved traumas are deep wounds that create raw spots that are particularly difficult to work through. It takes tremendous courage and vulnerability to express or speak about our traumas with others. Deep traumas often take professional attention and commitment. However, the EmC process can, at times, act as a clarifier of the need to seek professional help. Creating strong bonds with those we work with can be helpful for individuals who need to work through their particular past traumatic events. This happens because there is a feeling of safety. Creating safety in your team to express the three levels of emotions, and validating those emotions is a critical component in helping people gain the courage to share their experiences and emotions. The awareness of clues such as body language, ease, or difficulty of the conversation will allow us to better understand the emotional space occupied by each individual.

In moments of stress, different people manage the situation differently. Some are comfortable in staying in the present and dealing with the various factors causing the stress. They do this more or less adequately with conflicts in their working relationships. But, others are immediately thrown into the past, remembering a traumatic event similar to the one causing the current stress. The depth of this past trauma determines how long they wrestle with events, people, and emotions. As the EmC process has the long-term goal of creating and maintaining positive and sustainable interactions, it is critical that obstacles like past traumas are not put aside but rather broken down into pieces, allowing the individual to process them and even be empowered by their resilience. The process of recognizing raw spots and trigger points is critical when we encounter individuals with past traumatic events. In addition to being aware of individual challenges, awareness of contextual or structural anomalies in the workplace will determine the speed and the depth of the EmC integration as a holistic strategy. Even though the EmC strategy is not situational or content-driven, the contextual environment of the workplace is a key consideration in determining the right approach.

Organizations and teams that are suffering from financial loss or poor market conditions, poor structural foundations, or ineffective dynamics are not that different than an individual in a moment of conflict. As the individual is unable to move from their amygdala response to a more cognitively based set of reactions, so is the organization unable to create a healing environment in the middle of an existential crisis. As noted in Table 9.3, awareness of the organization's position is important in determining how well the EmC process will work as an organizational strategy. Fundamentally, the individual and the organization are both suffering from the weak emotional connections among people and teams. Awareness of past traumas, current context, and organizational situation gives an important tool in making the EmC process into the effective and sustainable strategy.

*Table 9.3 Emotional connection and increasing awareness*

| Challenge | Remedy |
|---|---|
| Awareness | • Accept that we need to be connected with each other<br>• Create strong emotional bonds<br>• Be attuned to cues<br>• Pay attention to past traumas |

# Independence

Being independent and acting strong is a cornerstone of our Western culture. It helps form our national identity and creates the framework for our organizations. As a result, within our companies, the responsibility for managing situations, conflicts, misunderstandings, and stressful events often falls on individuals. They are often expected to solve these problems alone, by themselves. Furthermore, we amplify this sense of independence by processes that minimize the importance of the emotional dependency that is inherently the basis of all relationships at work or elsewhere. In fact, we are highly dependent on people we work with—not just for content, but for the sense of safety and value that we all seek. A desire for independence, whether culturally driven or personally manifested during times of stress, prevents us from reaching out, asking for help, recognizing the emotional toll inside ourselves and others, or being empathic. We, inadvertently, create the perfect storm for further deterioration of already poor relationships. In situations where individuals who have repeatedly sought connection and understanding were instead consistently rejected by their colleagues, a sense of independence develops—albeit with its own dysfunctionalities—including anxiety and depression, which are manifested in subpar performance.

There is a fine line between managing our hurt emotions by ourselves and seeking others to help us regain our emotional balance. As we have discussed in previous chapters, we see how our raw spots are triggered and how our protective behaviors impact our relationships. If we are able to regulate our triggers and thereby our responses so as to remain connected in a positive cycle, then we no longer feel alone and disconnected. Reaching out for help, sharing our emotional state and experience, and risking being vulnerable is difficult but important. We have to teach ourselves to see these actions not as weaknesses, but rather as strengths that empower us to tackle the issues and arrive at better connections (see Table 9.4). At the organizational level, structures, workflow, and task distribution depend greatly on individual performance and abilities. As managers, we expect each person to know what they are doing and to do it well. We amplify this through our performance evaluations, which focus, for the most part, on individuals even when we evaluate teams. Leaders, on the other hand, recognize the importance of the underlying connections, which bind people together and the value of real teams that are dependent on each other and the magic they produce, achieving ambitious goals.

Table 9.4 *Emotional connection and building bonds*

| Challenge | Remedy |
| --- | --- |
| Independence | • Reach out for help<br>• Accept emotional support<br>• Know that sharing your emotional experience is a sign of strength |

## Vulnerability

The courage to be vulnerable is within all of us. How and when we seek this courage, feed it, and nurture it so that our true self shows itself at all times is something we struggle with all our life. The authentic self is not easy to achieve. Societal norms in many communities, both in the East and West, emphasize the importance of secrecy and emotional distance so as to measure each interaction before fully committing. We carry this sense of fear of sharing our emotions with us into our work situations.

As we gain experiences, we either confirm or modify this behavior based on the feedback we get from our important relationships. Unfortunately, the more impenetrable we make ourselves, the more distance we put between us and those we depend on or wish to have productive relationships with us. As our biological desire rests in close connections, we simply hurt ourselves further and further with each act of closure.

Vulnerability or being open with how we feel about something or someone has the beauty of bringing us closer to those we depend on and care about. Vulnerability acts like a magnet that pulls people closer, giving us a chance to engage them openly and honestly. It brings a level of authenticity to interactions that create the dialogue so essential to repairing hurts and building durable bonds. The EmC process depends greatly on an authentic exchange of feelings and emotions between all participants. As such, anyone who brings with them the notion of *standoffishness* can significantly halt the progress. The desire to not show one's vulnerability presents itself in aggressive, intimidating, and demeaning statements and approaches, especially at the beginning of the process. The tone of voice can also give us a clue because individuals who do not wish to engage often use a loud voice to communicate their disagreement with the process or why they are even there. We have all seen these people, but we know that behind their anger or dismissiveness lies a great deal of fear and protective behavior safeguarding their emotions. They are struggling because they are in pain from the connections that were lost during the conflict or the stress. In addition, and perhaps more importantly, for now, they are in an internal wrestling match with societal expectations refraining them from sharing emotions, experiences of past vulnerability, rejections and abandonments, and their biological desire to be vulnerable to seek attachment.

On the opposite side, the desire to be less vulnerable manifests itself in some people by pushing them to shut down. We often see with distressed teams the toxic and triggering nature of emotional shutdowns. It is very hard for most of us to really grasp how we can possibly threaten others by simply doing nothing, by staying silent, or distant. If we think of interaction as a dance, then shutting down is the same as leaving the dance floor, abandoning the others, making them feel alone. Research shows that habitually shutting people out in difficult conversations results in escalating relationship distress and the breakdown of trust and coop-eration.[4] As a result, stonewalling most often actually fires up anger and conflict rather than calming it down. This makes sense. We depend on each other. When there is no response, this stirs shock and helplessness in us. There is suddenly no relationship. We have no impact, and we are all alone. Emotional rejection from someone we depend on registers in our brain in the same way as physical pain; they are both traumatic in nature.[5]

Among the many different approaches in the EmC process, repetition becomes quite valuable in these situations. The facilitator or leader con-tinuously repeats encouraging and supportive phrases such as, "It makes sense you don't trust the process," "I can see that this is frustrating," or "I can see you are angry." These phrases allow individuals to feel that they are being heard and seen, and the artful switch from the statement to a question such as, "Are you angry at the moment?" allows us to begin to connect emotionally, letting the individual begin their journey into emotions, gaining authenticity along the way. While vulnerability needs courage, in a way, it also feeds courage by allowing us to take steps we would otherwise never take (see Table 9.5). It is the ultimate positive loop allowing the world to see our most authentic self, allowing us to be in a state of perpetual emotional balance.

*Table 9.5  Emotional connection and the power of vulnerability*

| Challenge | Remedy |
| --- | --- |
| Vulnerability | • Seek courage within yourself<br>• Stay present<br>• Give yourself a chance to repair your relationships |

## Questions for Reflection

In thinking about this chapter, here are some questions to consider:

1. In your experiences with your peers, bosses, and direct reports, please reflect the interactions that were unexpectedly negative or conten-tious and think through the challenges discussed in this chapter.

2. In particular, how would you rank the different challenges as to the causes of the conflict?

3. Staying with the same conflict or difficult situation, conversely, how do you see the presence of each of these components in arriving at a bonding conversation?

## Summary of Chapter 9

We discussed some of the common challenges in the workplace, which, under even the best circumstances, can interrupt or divert our positive interactions. Trust is essential for the team and organizational success. Lack of trust prevents us from having healthy and positive interactions and building trusting relationships. Without robust emotional connections, we form limited relationships, which are transactional at best and prone to rapid disengagement.

Alignment of values, expectations, and agendas is critical to business success. Misalignment or the perception of it can create significant obstacles for the development of a meaningful workplace connection. Becoming aware of how sensitive we can be when we work together sheds light on how easily we can become disconnected, hurt, and disengaged. It takes a great deal of courage and vulnerability to express or speak about our hurts, especially at the workplace. It is only when we feel emotionally safe that we share ourselves with the people we care about.

Being independent and acting strong is a cornerstone of our Western culture, forming both our national character and creating the basis for our organizational infrastructure. Reaching out for help, sharing our emotional state and experience, and risking being vulnerable are difficult but important steps in building our strength so that we can grow and thrive. Vulnerability pulls people closer and gives us a chance to engage openly and honestly. The courage to be vulnerable is within all of us.

Effectively addressing the challenges noted in this chapter, paves the way for a holistic strategy to integrate the EmC process into the organizational culture.

# CHAPTER 10

# Resilience and Thriving Cultures

Imagine your peers, direct reports, and boss coming to work every day full of energy, positivity, and shared purpose. Furthermore, imagine that no matter the obstacles or the contextual challenges, the basics of the organizational and individual interactions are firmly rooted in emotional connections. To someone looking in from the outside, they would describe the people as collaborative, engaged, and generally happy. A deeper inspection of such a workplace reveals a group of people who are compassionate, understanding, and supportive of each other—thereby creating the right environment for thriving.

## Emotions Are the Key

This is not a dream, nor is it an impractical objective. It is the result of acknowledging and addressing the role emotions play as the underlying and the overarching element in a flourishing organization. Mission, vision, and values are critical to success, and what assures that success are the people whose connections with each other must be strong and positive. The future of team performance lies in the ability to create a safe environment where people can openly share their ideas, take risks and fail, explore without blame, and collaborate inclusively and organically. Leadership during times of great uncertainty and volatility requires individual and organizational resilience, intelligence, and trust. The basis of all of these are people whose connections with each other are durable, especially during moments of stress.

## Lessons from Apollo 13

We all remember the scene from the movie *Apollo 13* when they informed Houston that they have a problem. In fact, the phrase "Houston, we have a problem" has become part of our vernacular. It is, however, the scene that unfolds at the Space Command Center, which demonstrates the point. This group of men at that moment in time with unbelievable stress on their shoulders did not attack, blame, or criticize each other. They did not create an environment where frustration, irritation, or confusion determined their actions. Instead, what took place were actions by a cohesive and determined group of individuals fully committed to solving a set of problems they had never before encountered. In this setting, we observed how each individual was valued for their role and knowledge. We saw and felt the pressure, but we also observed their continuous reassurance of each other and the belief in their ultimate success.

In many ways, this moment at the Space Command Center demonstrates how a thriving organization having emotionally connected individuals can respond effectively to unforeseen challenges. Most of us do not work at the Space Command Center, nor do we have the fate of a spaceship in our hands. However, as leaders, we have something far greater for which we are responsible: we must create and nurture an environment that values relationships, allowing every person to thrive. As leaders, we must understand and know the importance of balance not just within ourselves but also between that of organizational objectives and individual growth and vitality. As leaders, we are primarily the champions for the *people* part of organizations. This requires us to stretch beyond the content or contextual relationships and dive deeper into the emotional underpinnings of the connections we wish to make.

EmC is a strategy for all people who see themselves as leaders within and of their organizations. It is a management tool when we need to solve conflicts or improve performance. But for leaders, it is a powerful strategy to help people reach the next level, giving them wings to fly. Flight can only happen when we have something solid to lift off from. EmC creates the solid platform we all need to achieve flight, and the depth of our connections gives us the safety net when we fall. The EmC strategy provides leaders with the ability to achieve both.

# Using EmC as a Proactive Strategy

In this book thus far, we have discussed the use of the EmC process to address conflicts, disconnections, and general moments of challenge within organizations. In these circumstances, the EmC process can work to address the emotional deficits and begin repairing the relationship. You may be wondering, is the EmC a tool only for when connections are broken, or can it be used prospectively and strategically to maintain and enhance positive cultures? While the majority of the work in the EmC process has been with teams with known difficulties or particular conflicts, the process itself is a positively oriented activity. It creates experiences everyone can draw from to nurture an emotionally supportive workplace. As you may recall, the process is heavily weighted toward discovering the negative emotions and protective behaviors leading to the bonding conversations, which have the potential of starting the positive cycle.

In a workplace that is experiencing little or no significant conflicts, the EmC can work as a strategy to dramatically enhance current performance, both for individuals and teams. Sharing conversations such as in the EmC process, often center on emotional experiences, be they conflict-driven or, as we think prospectively, of thriving experiences. Most everyone has a particular situation or a time in mind when they felt as though they were thriving. They describe these situations as a time where they experienced a series of positive emotions, which were empowering. Consider the following example Ramin provided from his experience.

*We had a group of nine individuals, all leaders, all with opinions, and all with a great deal of power. We met on a regular basis and, over time, had built a thriving environment where everyone felt heard, empowered, and supported. From time to time, one member's term would be up, and they would leave to be replaced by a brand-new person. Our overall team was so emotionally strong that the new individual would immediately find themselves in a positive and supportive environment. This was a time when we were really thriving and could accomplish anything. In fact, we did accomplish many objectives that were thought to be impossible to achieve.*

This example helps us to recognize how important it is for teams to focus on thriving situations and to learn from them, empowering team members to grow, create, and blossom. By focusing on the elements in the thriving situation, we can explicitly acknowledge the critical factors necessary for thriving to have occurred in the first place. In a thriving culture, disconnects exist and do occur. However, the culture itself and its positive orientation have the power to guide people into a positive cycle as they focus on reconnection. The EmC, both in its conflict resolution form and in its prospective orientation, is an essential strategy throughout the lifespan of any organization.

## Nurturing Extraordinary Professional Growth

Professional growth is a goal for all of us as we find it exciting to face new challenges, testing our skills and capacity. Sometimes, growth is measured in our ability to secure higher positions, and at other times, it is seen as our ability to tackle unprecedented problems. Whichever form it takes, taking risks, collaborating with people whom we would normally not engage, and expressing ideas we may have thought controversial are the key elements to creativity and ensuring continued growth. It is well documented that we have an innate need to grow and develop our skills and abilities.[1] In situations when we are prevented from growing, we become anxious and soon thereafter find ourselves increasingly disconnected and eventually disengaged from the workplace.[2] Interestingly, most people would agree that the presence of a professionally growing environment can immediately begin to reverse the disconnection and disengagement.

It has been said that success is predicated on three essential elements: talent, passion, and hard work. Without the presence of all of these and in harmony with each other, one is simply just good. When these elements are in full sync (Figure 10.1) and are connected to each other through strong emotional connection spread out through the organization, pockets of extraordinary outcomes become possible.

To achieve extraordinary professional growth, individuals need powerful motivation. Best-selling motivation author Daniel Pink, when

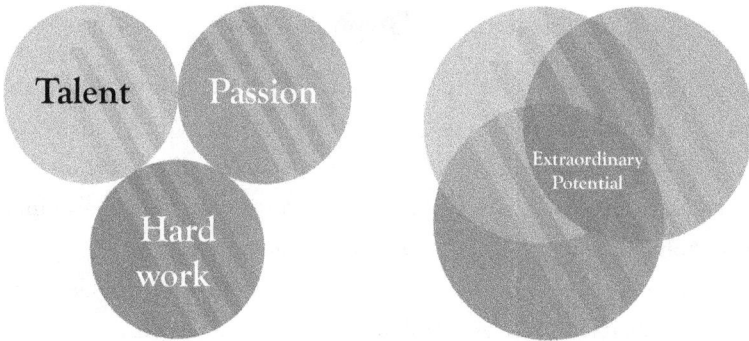

*Figure 10.1 The intersection of talent, passion, and hardwork*

examining thriving companies and work cultures, has found that individuals have three primary intrinsic motivators: autonomy, mastery, and necessity.[3] The science of emotional connection and the importance of creating and nourishing positive emotions at work directly support Pink's ideas. A positive environment allows individuals to feel valued and thus have a strong sense of feeling needed. They are able to grow and gain mastery, and by functioning from a high level of emotional safety, they have the opportunity to be autonomous. These individuals achieved geometric growth.

People who are emotionally connected attribute the following remarks to the future of their work:

- *Increased productivity*
- *Cohesive work environment*
- *Better quality of life*
- *Thriving culture*
- *Greater engagement*
- *Increased creativity*
- *Improved trust*
- *Supportive environment*
- *Happiness at work*
- *Approach work with enthusiasm*
- *Greater motivation*

- *More fun*
- *More collaborative*
- *Improved innovation*
- *Make better decisions*
- *Fearless*
- *More transparent*
- *More energy*
- *Sustain through obstacles*
- *More confident*
- *Listen better*

## Thriving Through Flow

The concept of flow is described in psychology as a state where we are creative, productive, and happy, unaware of time or external stressors.[4] Athletes, musicians, creative artists have the easiest time pointing to moments of flow. Leaders and individuals in organizations can also find these moments when they reflect on thriving situations.

Positive emotional connections and strong bonds are the elements critical for people to reach their state of flow within organizations. Our attempts at reconnections and re-engagements are not to simply create a productive working environment. They are the basis from which stronger connections and emotional engagements can occur—thus potentially leading to a greater flow within organizations. The deeper our understanding of emotional connection, our knowledge of ourselves, and how our brains function during stress, the more we have the power to push through and grow, creating stronger bonds. It is such moments that give brilliance to us and our teams at work. We have, therefore, reframed the culture in a way that induces, encourages, and nurtures optimism and growth.

Throughout this book, we have illustrated the experiential nature of the EmC process using Linda's team. While she and her team made significant progress in reconnecting through the process, it is the learned experiences that will carry them through as they face new situations. Having gone through the process, they would have learned the facial cues, the triggering statements, and their emotional responses to the degree that allows them to recognize these signs quickly and to address them explicitly, leading to minimal disconnection time. Eventually, emotionally connected team members work through conflicts in a fluid and natural manner. The language of EmC gives us the words and actions to help individuals gain and maintain emotional balance, leading to individual and community thriving.

## Nurturing Innovation

Traditionally, organizations were created to promote stability and predictability through hierarchy, silos, and differentiation of work. These types of structures do well in an environment of certainty with known outcomes and defined measures. On the other hand, when it comes to times of uncertainty and a rapidly changing environment, agile organizations offer adaptive, resilient, and innovative structures focused on evolving objectives. These organizations achieve stability in a dynamic culture.

Emotional connections are the basis upon which organizations can create an exciting duality of having the stability for consistency and quality and the dynamism that allows for market competitiveness. Anthony Robbins, who has extensively researched the motivating factors essential for people who perform complex functions, categorizes these into the following: *certainty; uncertainty or variety; significance; connection; growth; and contribution (meaning or purpose).*[5] Financial incentives or power dynamics do not even make the list. They are not unimportant, but his research shows that after a certain minimum amount of salary and job security, they are no longer motivators. An emotionally connected workplace exhibits the key ingredients of safety, value, and care for people to be open and honest, to receive feedback that honors their vulnerability, and to feel that their leaders understand their feelings.

The importance of consistency and predictability is well understood. In terms of brain structure, this is when the amygdala is literally at peace, allowing for the cognition part of the brain to understand and evaluate the external environment for new opportunities and connections. Forming strong emotional attachments at the workplace allows for the appreciation of variety, as it brings new possibilities and positive motivations. People become more open to new ideas and to take risks and explore. In addition, being of value to others is paramount in forming healthy relationships that endure during stressful situations. It is the sense of being useful, being important, and being needed gives us the motivation to nurture a positive self-image. Equally important, it pulls people closer, providing emotional satisfaction, reinforcing our attachment-oriented needs.

The famous example of the janitor in NASA illustrates the culmination of strong emotional connections and the presence of the key motivators. In a late-night encounter between President Lyndon B. Johnson and a janitor before the launch of Apollo 11, a smiling and happy janitor was asked what he was doing there so late at night, and why was he so happy given the job of being a janitor? He responded, "Why shouldn't I be happy? I have a great job, and I am helping put a man on the moon."

This level of ownership represents the power of connections. The goal of every leader is to create and nurture positive places of work where business objectives are met—but more importantly, the ingredients necessary for innovation, creativity, and growth are present and in abundance.

As you strive to achieve your own *moon shot*, we know the power of emotional connection, and using the EmC process as a strategy will guide your journey, providing the pathway to success.

# Appendix A

## List of Raw Spots

1. Being excluded or rejected
2. Not being valued or appreciated for your work, skills, or performance
3. Having an ambition or dream that other people are not interested in or seem to doubt your ability to achieve
4. Not acknowledging the point you are making
5. When someone turns away from you
6. Criticizing or making jokes about something fundamental to who you are
7. Being told your feelings are not valid or reasonable
8. A show of disapproval or disgust from someone close to you
9. Dislikes you or views you negatively
10. Communicating your needs and getting ignored, minimized, or criticized
11. Being judged as not good enough or not as good as someone else
12. When someone is trying to change you or make you into something you are not
13. Someone close to you is telling you that you do not deserve something
14. Someone is making demeaning comments about you
15. Someone close to you is being aggressive or intimidating toward you
16. Ignoring your questions, the importance of your questions, or ignoring your comments

# Appendix B

## List of Negative Emotions

| Surface emotions | Softer emotions | Primary emotions |
|---|---|---|
| ☐ Frustrated | ☐ Worried | ☐ Fear |
| ☐ Annoyed | ☐ Shaky | ☐ Sadness |
| ☐ Irritated | ☐ Isolated | ☐ Shame |
| ☐ Shut down | ☐ Unimportant | ☐ Surprise |
| ☐ Resentful | ☐ Dismissed | |
| ☐ Frozen or | ☐ Let Down | |
|    numb | ☐ Helpless | |
| ☐ Upset | ☐ Hopeless | |
| ☐ Disturbed | ☐ Hurt | |
| ☐ Tense | ☐ Panicked | |
| ☐ Disappointed | ☐ Intimidated | |
| ☐ Betrayed | ☐ Overwhelmed | |
| ☐ Angry | ☐ Inadequate | |
| ☐ Confused | ☐ Rejected | |
| ☐ Alone | ☐ Abandoned | |
| ☐ Exhausted | ☐ Failing | |
| | ☐ Embarrassed | |
| | ☐ Defeated | |
| | ☐ Not heard | |
| | ☐ Not valued | |
| | ☐ Desperate | |

# Appendix C

## List of Positive Emotions

- [ ] Happy
- [ ] Connected
- [ ] Safer/Secure
- [ ] Appreciated
- [ ] Important
- [ ] Valued
- [ ] Satisfied
- [ ] Relieved
- [ ] Confident
- [ ] Enthusiastic
- [ ] Free
- [ ] Stronger
- [ ] Hopeful
- [ ] Optimistic
- [ ] Motivated
- [ ] Not Alone
- [ ] Relaxed
- [ ] Refreshed
- [ ] Energized
- [ ] Grateful

# Appendix D

# Want to Do a Deeper Dive into the Emotional Connection Training?

To further your knowledge and skills the EmC process, there are three online courses available: EmC Basic Course, EmC Master Class, and EmC Train the Trainer Certification. Each course will provide you with tools, knowledge, and understanding through the instructional videos, exercises, practical tools, resources, and demonstrations through recorded sessions.

For more information, please visit emcleaders.com or send an e-mail to emc@emcleaders.com.

# Interviews With Leaders Who Use the EmC Process

## Alejandro Tocigl, CEO of Miroculus

*Our biggest challenge was to understand human to human disconnects as a negative cycle that often comes from only good intentions, but that can be detrimental to an organization if it can't be isolated and addressed from an emotional perspective.*

*It is very hard to navigate through difficult times when you are not able to immediately address and repair all those negative cycles that occur between two or more team members. It feels like you are losing the battle within your own team.*

*The EmC process gave us tools to connect between one and the other at an emotional level while being able to isolate, address, and repair negative cycles within our team. At the end of the day, we are all emotional beings and are our emotions very often driving our decisions. Understanding each other at that level helps to build honest relationships and a much more cohesive team.*

*Our team has learned a new language and approach to emotions and emotional connection. This has allowed us to express ourselves from the most vulnerable and honest dimension, helping us to better understand each other. We have also seen that every disconnect is an opportunity to increase bonding between each other if addressed correctly.*

*At our company, we aim to help to create better leaders, and this is a tool every leader should know about. I would tell people to give it a try. It is like opening the door to honesty, vulnerability, and deeper human connection. These are incredibly powerful tools for increased team bonding and performance.*

## Richard J. Ward, Chairman of the Board of Governors at the Center Club Orange County

*Learning to appreciate the feelings and needs of my board members was my biggest challenge. It made me feel frustrated, as I was not able to always communicate effectively with them.*

*After learning the EmC process, I have closer relationships with most board members and much more effective communications.*

*I am now able to readily have personal conversations with formerly distant board members. I get my phone calls returned promptly with the intention of learning why I wanted to speak to the individual.*

*This part of human interactions is extremely important and is not generally a part of most leaders' training or natural abilities.*

*This is not a short-term fix for bad relationships, but rather a new way to approach relationships that will bring everyone closer if regularly practiced over time.*

## Sam W. Girgis, MBM, Training and Development Specialist, ATD-OC Member

*My absolute biggest challenge prior to learning/using the EmC process was communication amongst new hires. This was a challenge because not everyone has the exact background for office administration or office management, as well as being able to multi-task and focus on medical devices.*

*Therefore communication was essential, and EmC helped me understand and apply emotional intelligence better in the workplace as it relates to self-management, leadership, and awareness of how others perceive me and how I can communicate effectively to them.*

*The challenge allowed me to put myself in others' shoes and understand that everyone learns differently and that training is essential as it is, at times, is not the only aspect of helping a company grow. It is also communicating with coworkers and seeing what challenges they are going through, and helping them to build on more skills.*

*The changes that came about after I learned the EmC process was a better understanding of the needs of my co-workers, how to be more patient with them through the learning process, and also how to lead by example by putting myself in their shoes when I was a new hire at the company at one point.*

*Specific results that I saw were better teamwork on the medical devices, being able to increase revenue collectively, allowing others to take the lead, and being able to learn from others as well in their abilities and skills, and how we can communicate more effectively. EmC allowed me to understand [what it is like] . . . to work in other people's shoes more than anything, and [it] has given me the foundation to be able to be a better leader by communicating better with co-workers.*

*From my personal experience, I saw EmC was very effective and very applicable in its principles. It is highly recommended in the areas of [improving] emotional intelligence, leadership, communication, training, and developing employees as well as employers. It also helps communication between managers and any of the employees they are managing. It is worth learning, and it also earns continuing education credits that help in the development of the company and its employees.*

*EmC was a great learning experience, [including] the quality of the material, the videos, content, and depth of the product. The experience is great for any company developing its employees into leaders and expanding its training. This is [a tool for understanding] organizational behavior at its best.*

## Others Leaders and EmC Champions

*As a leader, EmC helped me to bring a framework in order to create a greater understanding between our team members about each other's strengths, beliefs, and perspectives. As a result, we have become even more effective, collaborative, and connected.*

—Dawn Reese, CEO, The Wooden Floor

*The ROI on this training is exponential! All of the people we interact with—bosses, peers, direct reports, clients, and family members—experience EmC benefits from the individual who engages in this process.*

—Irakli (Rocky) Bandzeladze,
Executive Vice President, Banking

*I took the EmC training and immediately had an opportunity to utilize it with a Leadership Team. I encourage anyone interested in improving personal or workplace relationships to take this training. It will truly make a difference!*

—Lois Carson, Executive Coach

# Notes

## Chapter 1

1. "Psychological Safety, Emotional Intelligence, and Leadership in a Time of Flux." 2020.
2. (CPP Global Human Capital Report 2008)
3. (Mikulincer and Shaver 2009)
4. (Iacoboni 2008)
5. (Mikulincer and Shaver 2016)
6. (Bowlby 1944)
7. (Bowlby 1969)
8. (Bowlby 1969)
9. (Rogers 1961)
10. (Minuchin and Fishman 1981)
11. (Elliott, et al. 2004)
12. (Arnold 2020)
13. (Goleman 1996)

## Chapter 2

1. (Mikulincer and Shaver 2016)
2. The term, bonding conversations, is primarily used in improving relationships between individuals.
3. Psychologist Jeffry Simpson leads Social Interaction Lab at the University of Minnesota where they study and observe behaviors in adults during stressful situations and link to a person's attachment style, evaluated from their relationship history, present expectations, and their way of dealing with their emotions.
4. (Bowlby 1988)

## Chapter 3

1. If you want to watch the experiment, *Still Face Experiment*, you can find it on YouTube https://youtube.com/watch?v=apzXGEb-Zht0&t=31s

2. (Isaacson n.d.)

3. (Mikulincer 1995)

4. (Stenberg, Wiking, and Dahl 1998)

5. (Logothetis et al. 2001)

6. (Eisenberger, Lieberman, and Williams 2004)

## Chapter 4

1. (Scherer and Eckman 1984)

2. (Gibaldi and Cusack 2019)

3. (Carder 2019)

4. (Scherer, Shorr, and Johnstone 2001)

## Chapter 5

1. (LeDoux 1998)

2. (Panksepp 1998)

3. (Franz and Ewing 1980)

4. (Johnson 2019)

5. (Kobak, et al. 1998)

6. The term, freeze and flee "tango," was first introduced by Susan Johnson (2008) representing individuals who are shut down in responses to the stress in their relationship

7. (Thomson and Johnson 2006)

8. (Paulssen 2009)

9. (Brown 2015)

10. (Eldad and Mario 2003)

11. (Bowlby 1982)

12. (Şchiopu 2015)

13. (Gable, Gonzaga and Strachman 2006)

## Chapter 6

1. (Mikulincer and Shaver 2016)

2. (Simpson, Rholes, and Nelligan 1992)

3. (Johnson, et al. 2013)

4. (Ainsworth, et al. 1978)

5. (Davidovitz, et al. 2007)
6. (Johnson 2008)
7. (Lieberman 2013)
8. (Gross and Thompson 2007)
9. (LeDoux 1996)
10. (Gibaldi and Cusack 2019)

## Chapter 7

1. (Mayer, Salovey and Caruso 2008)
2. (Bowlby 1973)

## Chapter 8

1. (Mino 2017)
2. (Mayer, et al. 2003)

## Chapter 9

1. (Yip et al. 2018)
2. (Ashkanasy and Dorris 2017)
3. (Barreiro and Treglown 2020)
4. (Smith, et al. 2003)
5. (Eisenberger, Lieberman, and Williams 2004)

## Chapter 10

1. (Rogers, Lyon, and Tausch 2013)
2. (Ashkanasy and Dorris 2017)
3. Daniel H. Pink is the author of six provocative books about business and human behavior.
4. (Csikszentmihalyi 1990)
5. Anthony Robbins has conducted live seminars attended by more than four million people. Mr. Robbins has empowered more than 50 million people from 100 countries through his audio, video, and life training programs

# References

"Psychological Safety, Emotional Intelligence, and Leadership in a Time of Flux." 2020. McKinsey Insights, July, N.PAG. https://search-ebscohost-com. proxy1.ncu.edu/login.aspx?direct=true&db=bth&AN=144370685&site=eds-live

A definition of Emotional Intelligence as described in Mayer, J.D., P. Salovey, D.R. Caruso, and G. Sitarenios. 2003. "Measuring Emotional Intelligence with the MSCEIT V2.0." *Emotion* 3, no. 1, pp. 97–105.

Ainsworth, M.D.S., M.C. Blehar, E. Waters, and S. Wall. 1978. *Patterns of Attachment: A Psychological Study of the Strange Situation.* Oxford: Lawrence Erlbaum.

All these styles are further described in Mikulincer, M., and P.R. Shaver. 2016. *Attachment in Adulthood: Structure, Dynamics, and Change*, 2nd ed. New York, NY: Guilford Press.

Anthony Robbins has conducted live seminars attended by more than four million people. Mr. Robbins has empowered more than 50 million people from 100 countries through his audio, video, and life training programs.

Arnold, S. 2020. "A Quantitative Descriptive-Comparative Study: The Relationship Between Emotional Intelligence And Workplace Diversity." *The Sciences and Engineering* 81, nos. 2–B.

Ashkanasy, N.M., and A.D. Dorris. 2017. "Emotions in the Workplace." *Annual Review of Organizational Psychology & Organizational Behavior* 4, p. 67.

Barreiro, C.A., and L. Treglown. 2020. "What Makes an Engaged Employee? A Facet-Level Approach to Trait Emotional Intelligence as a Predictor of Employee Engagement." *Personality and Individual Differences* 159.

Bowlby, J. 1944. "Forty-Four Juvenile Thieves: Their Characters And Home Life." *International Journal of Psychoanalysis* 25, pp. 19–52.

Bowlby, J. 1969. *Attachment and Loss, Vol. 1. Attachment.* New York, NY: Basic Books.

Bowlby, J. 1969. *Attachment and Loss, Vol. 1. Loss,* 194. New York, NY: Basic Books.

Bowlby, J. 1973. *Attachment and Loss: Vol. 2. Separation: Anxiety and Anger.* New York, NY: Basic Books.

Bowlby, J. 1982. *Attachment and loss: Vol. 1. Attachment,* 2nd ed. New York, NY: Basic Books (original work published 1969).

Bowlby, J. 1988. *A Secure Base.* New York, NY: Basic Books.

Brown, B. 2015. *Daring Greatly: How the Courage to be Vulnerable Transforms the Way we Live, Love, Parent, and Lead,* 33–34. Penguin.

Carder, B. 2019. "Joy in the Workplace is a Business Advantage." *The Journal for Quality and Participation* 42, no. 1, pp. 25–27.

CPP Global Human Capital Report. 2008. "Workplace Conflict and How Businesses can Harness it to Thrive." CPP, Mountain View, CA.

Csikszentmihalyi, M. 1990. *Flow: The Psychology of Optimal Experience.* New York, NY: HarperCollins Publishers.

Daniel H. Pink is the author of six provocative books about business and human behavior.

Davidovitz, R., M. Mikulincer, P.R. Shaver, R. Izsak, and M. Popper. 2007. "Leaders as Attachment Figures: Leaders' Attachment Orientations Predict Leadership-Related Mental Representations and Followers' Performance and Mental Health." *Journal of Personality and Social Psychology* 93, no. 4, pp. 632–650.

Eisenberger, N.I., M.D. Lieberman, and K. Williams. 2004. "Why Rejection Hurts: A Common Neural Alarm System for Physical and Social Pain." *Trends in Cognitive Science* 8, pp. 294–300.

Eldad, R., and M. Mario. 2003. "Attachment Theory and Group Processes: The Association Between Attachment Style and Group-Related Representations, Goals, Memories, and Functioning." *Journal of Personality and Social Psychology* 6, p. 1220.

Elliott, R., J. Watson, R. Goldman, and L. Greenberg. 2004. *Learning Emotion-Focused Therapy: The Process Experiential Approach to Change.* Washington, DC: American Psychological Association.

fMRI is referred to as a functional magnetic resonance imaging that measures brain activity by detecting changes associated with blood flow. Studies show that when an area of the brain is in use, blood flow to that region also increases. Logothetis, N.K., J. Pauls, M. Auguth, T. Trinath, and A. Oeltermann. 2001. "A Neurophysiological Investigation of the Basis of the Bold Signal In fMRI." *Nature* 412, no. 6843, pp. 150–157.

Franz, A., and T. Ewing. 1980. *Psychoanalytic Therapy: Principles and Application.* Lincoln: University of Nebraska Press.

Gable, S.L., G.C. Gonzaga, and A. Strachman. 2006. "Will you be there for me when Things go Right? Supportive Responses to Positive Event Disclosures." *Journal of Personality and Social Psychology* 91, pp. 904–917.

Gibaldi, C., and G. Cusack. 2019. "Fear in the Workplace." *Review of Business* 39, no, 1, pp. 60–74.

Goleman, D. 1996. *Emotional Intelligence : Why It Can Matter More Than IQ.* New York, NY: Bantam Books.

Gross, J.J., and R.A. Thompson. 2007. "Emotion Regulation: Conceptual Foundations." In *Handbook of Emotion Regulation*, ed. J.J. Gross, 3–24. New York, NY: The Guilford Press.

Iacoboni, M. 2008. *Mirroring People: The New Science of How We Connect With Others.* New York, NY: Farrar, Straus and Giroux.

If you want to watch the experiment, *Still Face Experiment*, you can find it on YouTube https://youtube.com/watch?v=apzXGEbZht0&t=31s

Johnson, S. 2008. *Hold Me Tight: Seven Conversations for a Lifetime of Love*. New York, NY: The Little, Brown Spark of Hachette Book Group, Inc.

Johnson, S.M. 2019. *Attachment Theory in Practice: Emotionally Focused Therapy (EFT) with Individuals, Couples, And Families*. New York, NY: The Guilford Press.

Johnson, S.M., M. Burgess Moser, L. Beckes, A. Smith, T. Dalgleish, R. Halchuk, K. Hasselmo, P.S. Greenman, Z. Merali, and J.A. Coan. 2013. "Soothing the Threatened Brain: Leveraging Contact Comfort with Emotionally Focused Therapy." *PloS One* 8, no. 11, e79314.

Kobak, R., S. Duemmler, A. Burland, and E. Youngstrom. 1998. "Attachment and Negative Absorption States." *Journal of Systemic Therapies* 17, pp. 80–92.

LeDoux, J. 1996. *The Emotional Brain*, 1st ed. Simon & Schuster.

LeDoux, J. 1998. *The Emotional Brain: The Mysterious Underpinnings of Emotional Life*. Simon and Schuster.

Lieberman, M.D. 2013. *Social: Why Our Brains are Wired to Connect*. New York: Crown Publishers, Random House.

Mayer, J.D., P. Salovey, and D.R. Caruso. 2008. "Emotional Intelligence: New Ability or Eclectic Traits?" *The American Psychologist* 63, pp. 503–517.

Mikulincer, M. 1995. "Attachment Style and the Mental Representation of the Self." *Journal of Personality and Social Psychology* 69, pp. 1203–1215.

Mikulincer, M. and P.R. Shaver. 2016. *Attachment in Adulthood*, 2nd ed. New York, NY: Guilford Press.

Mikulincer, M., and P.R. Shaver. 2009. "An Attachment and Behavioral Systems Perspective On Social Support." *Journal of Social and Personal Relationships* 26, pp. 7–19.

Mikulincer, M., and P.R. Shaver. 2016. *Attachment in Adulthood: Structure, Dynamics, and Change*, 2nd ed. New York, NY: Guilford Press.

Mino, L. 2017. "Good Genes Are Nice, But Joy Is Better." *Harvard Gazette*, https://news.harvard.edu/gazette/story/2017/04/over-nearly-80-years-harvard-study-has-been-showing-how-to-live-a-healthy-and-happy-life/ (accessed August 10, 2020).

Minuchin, S., and H.C. Fishman. 1981. *Techniques of Family Therapy*. Cambridge, MA: Harvard University Press.

Panksepp, J. 1998. *Affective Neuroscience: The Foundations of Human and Animal Emotions*. New York, NY: Oxford University Press.

Paulssen, M. 2009. "Attachment Orientations in Business-to-Business Relationships." *Psychology & Marketing* 26, no. 6, pp. 507–533.

Psychologist Jeffry Simpson leads Social Interaction Lab at the University of Minnesota where they study and observe behaviors in adults during stressful situations and link to a person's attachment style, evaluated from their relationship history, present expectations, and their way of dealing with their emotions.

Rogers, C.R. 1961. *On Becoming a Person. Boston.* Houghton Mifflin.

Rogers, C.R., H.C. Lyon, and R. Tausch. 2013. *On Becoming an Effective Teacher—Person-centered Teaching, Psychology, Philosophy, and Dialogues with Carl R. Rogers and Harold Lyon.* London: Routledge.

Scherer, K.R., and P. Eckman, P. 1984. *Approaches to Emotion.* New York, NY: Psychology Press.

Scherer, K.R., A. Shorr, and T. Johnstone. 2001. *Appraisal Processes in Emotion: Theory, Methods, Research.* Canary, NC: Oxford University Press.

Şchiopu, A.F. 2015. "Workplace Emotions and Job Satisfaction." *International Journal of Economic Practices & Theories* 5, no. 3, pp. 277–282.

Simpson, J.A., W.S. Rholes, and J.S. Nelligan. 1992. "Support Seeking and Support Giving Within Couples In an Anxiety Provoking Situation: The Role of Attachment Styles." *Journal of Personality and Social Psychology* 62, no. 3, pp. 434–446.

Smith, E.R., J. Murphy, S. Coats, E. Rom, and M. Mikulincer. 2003. "Attachment Theory and Group Processes: The Association Between Attachment Style and Group-Related Representations, Goals, Memories, and Functioning." *Journal of Personality and Social Psychology* 84, pp. 1220–1235.

Stenberg, G., S. Wiking, and M. Dahl. 1998. "Judging Words at Face Value: Interference in a Word Processing Task Reveals Automatic Processing of Affective Facial Expressions." *Cognition & Emotion* 12, no. 6, pp. 755–782.

Steve Jobs stonewalled his board for months as described in the book, Isaacson, W. n.d. *Steve Jobs: The Exclusive Biography.* New York, NY: Simon & Schuster.

The term, bonding conversations, is primarily used in improving relationships between individuals.

The term, freeze and flee "tango," was first introduced by Susan Johnson (2008) representing individuals who are shut down in responses to the stress in their relationship.

Thomson, M., and A.R. Johnson. 2006. "Marketplace and Personal Space: Investigating the Differential Effects of Attachment Style Across Relationship Contexts." *Psychology & Marketing*, 23, pp. 711–726.

Yip, J., K. Ehrhardt, H. Black, and D.O. Walker. 2018. "Attachment Theory at Work: A Review and Directions For Future Research." *Journal of Organizational Behavior* 39, no. 2, pp. 185–198.

# About the Authors

**Dr. Lola Gershfeld,** Founder of EmC Leaders, is a board and team dynamics specialist, organizational psychologist, and thought leader in her field. She works with for-profit and not-for-profit organizations to create positive dynamics where team relationships are repaired, bonds are formed, and change happens to foster sustainable growth and ignite innovative potential.

Dr. Gershfeld developed the Emotional Connection (EmC) process, a groundbreaking and empirically supported approach to engage team members, resolve conflict, and build trust. EmC has been adapted and developed into education programs and certification courses that are accredited by the International Coaching Federation (ICF), Human Resources Certification Institute (HRCI), and Society of Human Resources and Management (SHRM) for recertification hours.

Dr. Gershfeld leads several EmC research projects with a group of scientists and business professionals who focus on demonstrating the effectiveness of the EmC methodology, content, and delivery through substantive research informed by best practices in psychology. She has written two other books the Effective Board and Team Dynamics Guide and TRUSTMAKERS. Her articles on the importance of emotional connection and leadership appear in *Forbes, The Corporate Board, Industry Week, Corporate Board Member, The CEO Magazine, Chief Executive Magazine, NACD Directorship, California CEO Magazine, Training Industry,* and others.

Dr. Gershfeld loves her work and wants everyone to know how to tune into emotions, not just to achieve their goals but to shape their relationship to thrive. She spends much of her time training people and sharing her knowledge through writing and speaking. When she is not working, she spends her time reflecting in hot yoga classes, exploring with her adorable five grandkids in Hawaii, and deepening her relationships with her life-partner, family, and colleagues.

**Ramin Sedehi**, Founder of Impact Human Learning, is focused on developing new learning models in the face of exponential change in the 21st century. He also serves as an integral member of Berkeley Research Group's Health Transformation Institute, seeking transformative interventions in health care, academic medicine, and the higher education industry.

Mr. Sedehi's work with EmC Leaders is centered on developing compassionate leadership and building thriving cultures within all types of organizations. He is particularly interested in applying the EmC strategy toward enabling community building and visionary leadership.

Mr. Sedehi has held leadership positions at several magnificent institutions such as UCSF, UCSF Stanford Health Care (USHC), University of Pennsylvania (Penn), American University of Beirut (AUB), and Weill Cornell Medicine-Qatar (WCMQ). In his three-plus decades of senior and executive service, he has grown as a leader, thinker, and intrapreneur.

As an award-winning faculty member at Penn, Mr. Sedehi regularly taught graduate courses in leadership, financial management, and complex organizations. His students have gone into leadership positions in the public and private sectors.

Mr. Sedehi is committed to enabling courageous leadership by helping leaders fundamentally, embrace love: love of ideas that move and inspire, love of people and their individual and collective aspirations, and love of doing and being in service.

When he is not working, Mr. Sedehi is an avid runner, tackling distances and terrains; he is driven to explore the limits; where the mind can go no further, and the heart takes over. He actively mentors others in long-distance running, professional endeavors, and life coaching, whatever it takes to empower change. He has also undertaken the genuinely humbling experience of writing a novel, bringing new dimensions of creativity into his work.

# About EmC Leaders

EmC Leaders is a leading organization committed to understanding, researching, and providing Emotional Connection (EmC) programs, specially designed for leaders, teams, boards, and individuals to improve their effectiveness.

Organizations that incorporate emotional connections (the EmC strategy) report improvements in engagement, create an inclusive and effective team culture, and exhibit higher productivity and performance. Our scientifically proven method is easy to use, based on rigorous research, and includes our proprietary tools and techniques. Our training programs and coaching services ensure effective skills are applied immediately. Our EmC strategy is a groundbreaking approach and pathway for organizations to thrive.

**Our Vision:** To unleash the human potential through the pleasure of growing and discovery. Build resilient teams through strong working relationships. Nurture thriving cultures through durable emotional bonds. We want people at work to feel happy, engaged, and connected.

**Our Mission:** To provide high-quality EmC programs and sessions to educate leaders, managers, teams, boards, human resource professionals, organizational development trainers, and consultants on the power of emotional connection. We seek to be change-makers, illuminating the essential role of emotions, and creating connected and flourishing communities.

**Our Values:**

- We value the human potential to elevate the human experience.
- We value research and practice as partners in informing our thoughts and actions.
- We value and respect the emotional state of every person.
- We value the independence of each person we work with and their individual journey.
- We value what we teach and do what we say.

**Our Motto:** Our diversity is our strength. Our work is local, but our impact is global. Our collaboration empowers us, and together, we are making the world a better place.

For more information, please visit, emcleaders.com.

# Index

## OTHER TITLES IN THE HUMAN RESOURCE MANAGEMENT AND ORGANIZATIONAL BEHAVIOR COLLECTION

- *The Successful New CEO* by Christian Muntean
- *Agility* by Michael Edmondson
- *Strengths Oriented Leadership* by Matt L. Beadle
- *Leadership In Disruptive Times* by Sattar Bawany
- *Level-Up Leadership* by Michael J. Provitera
- *The Truth About Collaborating* by Dr. Gail Levitt
- *Uses and Risks of Business Chatbots* by Tania Peitzker
- *Three Key Success Factors for Transforming Your Business* by Michael Hagemann
- *Hiring for Fit* by Janet Webb
- *Successful Recruitment* by Stephen Amos
- *Breakthrough* by Saundra Stroope
- *Transforming the Next Generation Leaders* by Sattar Bawany
- *What Millennials Really Want From Work and Life* by Yuri Kruman
- *Women Leaders* by Sapna Welsh and Caroline Kersten
- *Uniquely Great* by Lucy English
- *The Relevance of Humanities to the 21st Century Workplace* by Michael Edmondson
- *Untenable* by Gary Covert

## Announcing the Business Expert Press Digital Library

*Concise e-books business students need for classroom and research*

This book can also be purchased in an e-book collection by your library as

- a one-time purchase,
- that is owned forever,
- allows for simultaneous readers,
- has no restrictions on printing, and
- can be downloaded as PDFs from within the library community.

Our digital library collections are a great solution to beat the rising cost of textbooks. E-books can be loaded into their course management systems or onto students' e-book readers. The **Business Expert Press** digital libraries are very affordable, with no obligation to buy in future years. For more information, please visit **www.businessexpertpress.com/librarians**. To set up a trial in the United States, please email **sales@businessexpertpress.com**.

www.ingramcontent.com/pod-product-compliance
Lightning Source LLC
Chambersburg PA
CBHW061321220326
41599CB00026B/4980